A QUESTION OF FACT

by Wynyard Browne

SAMUEL FRENCH

Copyright © Wynyard Browne 1955. First published 1955, Reprinted 1958, 1964. All Rights Reserved

A QUESTION OF FACT is fully protected under the copyright laws of the British Commonwealth, including Canada, the United States of America, and all other countries of the Copyright Union. All rights, including professional and amateur stage productions, recitation, lecturing, public reading, motion picture, radio broadcasting, television, online/digital production, and the rights of translation into foreign languages are strictly reserved.

ISBN 978-0-573-13284-1

concordtheatricals.co.uk
concordtheatricals.com

FOR AMATEUR PRODUCTION ENQUIRIES

UNITED KINGDOM AND WORLD
EXCLUDING NORTH AMERICA
licensing@concordtheatricals.co.uk
020-7054-7298

Each title is subject to availability from Concord Theatricals, depending upon country of performance.

CAUTION: Professional and amateur producers are hereby warned that *A QUESTION OF FACT* is subject to a licensing fee. The purchase, renting, lending or use of this book does not constitute a licence to perform this title(s), which licence must be obtained from the appropriate agent prior to any performance. Performance of this title(s) without a licence is a violation of copyright law and may subject the producer and/or presenter of such performances to penalties. Both amateurs and professionals considering a production are strongly advised to apply to the appropriate agent before starting rehearsals, advertising, or booking a theatre. A licensing fee must be paid whether the title is presented for charity or gain and whether or not admission is charged.

This work is published by Samuel French, an imprint of Concord Theatricals Ltd.

The Professional Rights in this play are controlled by Curtis Brown, Haymarket House, 28 -29 Haymarket, London SW1Y 4SP.

No one shall make any changes in this title for the purpose of production. No part of this book may be reproduced, stored in a retrieval system, scanned, uploaded, or transmitted in any form, by any means, now known or yet to be invented, including mechanical, electronic, digital, photocopying, recording, videotaping, or otherwise, without the prior written permission of the publisher. No one shall share this title, or part of this title, to any social media or file hosting websites.

The moral right of Wynyard Browne to be identified as author of this work has been asserted in accordance with Section 77 of the Copyright, Designs and Patents Act 1988.

USE OF COPYRIGHTED MUSIC

A licence issued by Concord Theatricals to perform this play does not include permission to use the incidental music specified in this publication. In the United Kingdom: Where the place of performance is already licensed by the PERFORMING RIGHT SOCIETY (PRS) a return of the music used must be made to them. If the place of performance is not so licensed then application should be made to PRS for Music (www.prsformusic.com). A separate and additional licence from PHONOGRAPHIC PERFORMANCE LTD (www.ppluk.com) may be needed whenever commercial recordings are used. Outside the United Kingdom: Please contact the appropriate music licensing authority in your territory for the rights to any incidental music.

USE OF COPYRIGHTED THIRD-PARTY MATERIALS

Licensees are solely responsible for obtaining formal written permission from copyright owners to use copyrighted third-party materials (e.g., artworks, logos) in the performance of this play and are strongly cautioned to do so. If no such permission is obtained by the licensee, then the licensee must use only original materials that the licensee owns and controls. Licensees are solely responsible and liable for clearances of all third-party copyrighted materials, and shall indemnify the copyright owners of the play(s) and their licensing agent, Concord Theatricals Ltd., against any costs, expenses, losses and liabilities arising from the use of such copyrighted third-party materials by licensees.

IMPORTANT BILLING AND CREDIT REQUIREMENTS

If you have obtained performance rights to this title, please refer to your licensing agreement for important billing and credit requirements.

A Question of Fact

This play was first presented, after a short provincial tour, at the Piccadilly Theatre, London, on 10th December, 1953, with the following cast:—

NANNIE	Maureen Delany
NINA TRAFFORD	Mary Hinton
RACHEL GARDINER	Pamela Brown
PAUL GARDINER	Paul Scofield
CHARLES TRAFFORD	Henry Hewitt
ARTHUR LAMB	Harold Scott
GRACE SMITH	Gladys Cooper

The play was directed by FRITH BANBURY *with setting by* REECE PEMBERTON

The action of the play takes place in an English country town, in the sitting-room of a house which has been occupied for many years by a succession of married masters from a neighbouring public school.

ACT ONE
An evening in early May, a day or two before the beginning of the summer term.

ACT TWO
SCENE 1. Morning. Two months later.
SCENE 2. Late afternoon. Four weeks later, near the end of term.

ACT THREE
After dinner, the same evening.

No reference is intended, in this play, to any person, alive or dead.

NOTE: *The running time of this play, excluding intervals, is approximately two hours.*

NOTE TO PRODUCERS

I AM very grateful to two critics, Mr. Harold Hobson and Mr. J. C. Trewin, for perceiving what many people seem to have missed, that *A Question of Fact* is a play about imagination. This is the essential key to its satisfactory production.

Roughly, the shape of the play is this: In Act One we see Paul Gardiner's imagination (and to a lesser extent that of other characters) working, as it were, in a vacuum, with only a single disturbing clue. In Act Two we see the imagination confronted by the facts, objectively reported in a newspaper; and in Act Three we watch the final confrontation of the imagination with truth. The message of the play (and to those who like a play to have a message, I admit, for once, that this play actually has one) is that only by imagination can we grasp the truth about our fellow men but that, if it is not to mislead us, imagination must be used with love and not with fear. If this line is kept clearly in mind by the producer, the three rather odoriferous red herrings of murder, heredity and adoption should not unduly distract the audience's attention.

There is no doubt that, from the producer's point of view, the first act presents the greatest difficulties. I think it should start as cosily as possible, the normal happy return from the honeymoon but with something slightly wrong. When we have grasped what is wrong, we watch the couple continually tripping over this flaw in their happiness, picking themselves up and starting again, each time with a slight increase of underlying anxiety, until finally, at the curtain, the tension between them snaps and they are face to face with the threat of disaster.

The danger is, of course, that, unless each small crisis is sharply exposed and differentiated, this act may seem merely long and slow. For those who think it is long and slow anyway, there exists another version, swifter and more melodramatic, written for New York at the request of an American management and performed with success by some repertory companies in England. The publishers have kindly consented to make it available, on request, to any producer who feels that the first act needs a "gimmick".

But whichever version is used, the effectiveness of this act, and consequently of the whole play, depends largely on the actor playing Paul.

Two cardinal points in the character must be clearly brought out—that he is a man of powerful imagination and that he has a habit, when insecure or afraid, of defensive irony. We ought almost to *see* his imagination working; and there are many speeches in the part where this is possible. His irony, sometimes biting and savage, sometimes deceptively gay, always disconcerting to Rachel, is extremely important not only to the coherence of the character (it is almost the only overt sign, throughout most of the play, of his insecurity) but to the plot. For it is the irony with which Rachel finds it so difficult to deal; it is the irony which builds the barrier between them which ultimately terrifies her. A performance of Paul without irony could easily make nonsense of the play.

In the last act, when Mrs. Smith tells us about Ron—his charm, his imagination, his insecurity—we should feel that we are being told about what we have seen in Paul during the preceding acts.

The function of Mrs. Smith in the play is almost a dialectical one, of contradiction. She is the opposite of what we expect. She is surprising in the way in which life is always surprising compared with what one has imagined. She represents, as it were, the elements which the imagination overlooks, not only at her first entrance but throughout the last act. Just when we have decided that she is the brisk, witty, successful business-woman, we are startled to discover the depth of her feeling for Ron. Just when we think she is going to make a sentimental speech about capital punishment, she accepts it drily, realistically, almost with a shrug of the shoulders. This continual element in her of the unforeseen can prevent the long struggle between her and Paul in the last act from becoming a mere debate. It is important to remember that this struggle is inconclusive. When Mrs. Smith goes upstairs to bed, she is fully aware—and the audience should feel this, too—that the test of her success is yet to come, in the encounter between Paul and Rachel.

Paul's whole problem is, in a sense, a marital problem. If he "makes heavy weather", as one critic has said, of learning that his father was a murderer—how lightly, one gathers, some dramatic critics are accustomed to take catastrophic events in their own lives!—he does so largely because he makes this discovery when he is just about to marry, a time when the least introspective of men may tend to wonder, if only for a month or two, about the possible importance of family characteristics and habits, background, upbringing, heredity and so forth. Paul's most acute anxiety relates to Rachel.

Rachel's part therefore, though not showy, is of the utmost importance. She is the ordinary girl caught in an extraordinary situation. She is not a highbrow, a bohemian, a rebel or an artist. She is simple; in some ways, even conventional. Neither her intelligence nor her perception is out of the ordinary. She has no special equipment for dealing with the problem which confronts her except, as it turns out, the one thing needful—true love.

Her parents, whose concern for her welfare has set the ball of the plot rolling long before the play opens, can both very easily be misplayed. Mrs. Trafford is not simply the odious, possessive, interfering mother-in-law which is all that most people seem to see in her. In relation to the main theme, she is the woman without much imagination. Conventional and snobbish, her ambitions for her husband's career have been frustrated by his kindly, *laissez-faire* liberalism; and she regards any traces of a similar attitude of mind in Rachel as dangerous and liable to land her also in trouble. She is a nuisance but not a villain. Similarly, Charles Trafford is not an old booby who has forgotten all his Greek, which an actor out for laughs will tend to make him, but a representative of the liberal, humanist element in the English professional classes which still, perhaps despairingly, stands for civilization, in government offices, universities, law-courts and consulting rooms. It is their recognition of a common sense of values which is Charles Trafford's link with Paul as it is also Paul's link with Lamb.

Lamb, too, stands for civilization—embattled in a public-school common-room. If he is played as a dear, kind old bumbler, the point of the part is lost. Paul may describe him thus in a flash of self-defensive irony but he never really underestimates him; and it is only Nannie who dismisses him as eccentric. He is a man of real intellectual distinction, with a passion for the things of the mind. His insatiable interest in each new situation or person, amusing though it may be, is nevertheless that intellectual curiosity on which the advancement of civilization depends.

WYNYARD BROWNE.

N.B. Interleaved producer's copies of this play are available, price 10s. 6d. (postage 7d. extra), *direct from the publishers only*.

GARDEN BACKING

FRENCH WINDOWS

DESK

CUPBOARDS, Bookshelves over

BOOKCASE

HALL BACKING

TABLE LAMP

FIREPLACE

LAMP

ARMCHAIR

TABLE

SETTEE

STOOL

ARMCHAIR

ARMCHAIR

TABLE

* A QUESTION OF FACT

ACT ONE

An evening in early May, a day or two before the beginning of the summer term. The sitting-room of a small old house, vacated at the end of last term by a retiring public school master and not yet inhabited by the new tenants, though their furniture and books have been moved in. There is one door to the hall and a french window leading to the small garden. The room is pleasant, but dingy, and not yet organised. There are piles of books all over the place but not on the shelves; some still in packing cases. No loose covers are on the furniture. MRS. TRAFFORD *and* NANNIE *have been trying to get the place in some sort of order.*

When the curtain rises, MRS. TRAFFORD, *in the middle fifties, smart, sharp, country-housey, wearing good clothes, is standing* L. *of upstage crate, threading wire through curtains.*

NANNIE, *getting on for seventy, enters* U.C. *and pushes trolley above and by* R. *of sofa to below* L. *of armchair* R. *She is just about to lay supper for two, on a trolley by the electric fire.*

NANNIE. They'll have to have their supper in here to-night, the dining-room's all cluttered up with wedding presents . . . (*Puts up* L. *flap of trolley.*) And the coal didn't come yet : they'll have to do with this thing. (*Indicates electric fire.*) I expect they'll feel the cold after Italy.

(NANNIE *crosses above and by* R. *of trolley to switch* D.R. *below table. Pause. She glances at* MRS. TRAFFORD *and tries again.*)

Belongs to the College, doesn't it, this house? (NANNIE *crosses back to trolley, puts up* R. *flap, arranges small plates, napkins and rings.*) They ought to have had it re-decorated, to my way of thinking. Still, Miss Rachel'll soon have it looking nice. Remember how she used to be with her dolls' house? What them poor dolls used to suffer! Oh, it's grand to think of her married, isn't it, with a house of her own? (NANNIE *crosses above sofa and goes out* U.C., *returning with tray from* R. *end of table in hall.*)

MRS. TRAFFORD (*with a sigh*). Well, let's hope it turns out all right.

NANNIE (*glances at her; then, kindly*). You know, 'm, you worry too much. That's your trouble. You ought to be more like *his* mother.

---

* It is illegal to perform this play, *in any circumstances whatsoever*, without a licence. Please refer for full details to Copyright Notice preceding main text. *(Copyright Act 1956.)*

She's not the interfering type, Mrs. Gardiner. (*Puts tray on sofa, puts glasses and bread from tray on to trolley.*) I thought that at the wedding.

MRS. TRAFFORD. Well, there are reasons for that. Anyway, she's not his mother.

NANNIE (*amazed*). Not his mother?

MRS. TRAFFORD. Oh, hasn't Rachel told you? I thought everyone knew. No, he's only adopted.

NANNIE. Adopted? Well, I never . . . And there was I thinking I could catch a likeness! (*Still stunned by the news.*) Poor Mr. Gardiner though . . . Just fancy . . . Only adopted! (*Puts cruet and jug from tray on to trolley.*)

MRS. TRAFFORD. Perhaps you'll understand why we're so anxious when I tell you that . . . he comes from . . . well, a most unsatisfactory background. (*Picks up curtains from crate, crossing to below ladder at french windows.*)

NANNIE (*nodding, very worldly-wise, jumping to the inevitable conclusion*). Oh. I see . . . (*Crossing below sofa to between crates.* MRS. TRAFFORD *up ladder, hooks downstage end of curtains up.*) There, there, 'm, don't you worry. That don't make no difference. My sister-in-law at Clacton—you know, Carrie—she adopted a little boy just the same way. His mother was one of these rotten women. Carrie used to worry about him something dreadful. "Oh, Em, I'm frightened," she used to say, "what he'll be when he grows up"; but—do you know?—he's been better to her than many sons are, Len has . . .

(MRS. TRAFFORD *off steps, holding other end of curtains.* NANNIE *crosses, pulls ladder upstage of windows, steps back.*)

MRS. TRAFFORD. Yes, yes, I dare say, Nannie, but you see, in this case . . .

NANNIE. Of course, it's true, you never know with these adopted children. (MRS. TRAFFORD *up ladder, hooks on upstage end of curtains and centre hook.*) There were some people not far from where I lived when I was with Mrs. du Plessis. They adopted a little girl—and by the age of five she was getting money out of the lodgers to keep quiet and stop bothering. If they give her a penny or two, she'd be nice and quiet and smiling all morning. But if they wouldn't she'd make herself a regular little pest. Of course, she come of funny stock. Theatrical people her parents was—and then, years later, it come out in her. She went on the ice.

MRS. TRAFFORD. On the what?

NANNIE. Ice. "Rose Marie on ice," that's what she was in last. Beautiful skater she is, too. Funny how things seem to be in the blood. (*Moves away* C.)

MRS. TRAFFORD (*with a shudder*). Oh, don't ! (*Steps off ladder—tweaks curtains.*)

NANNIE (*glancing at her*). You've got nothing to worry about, 'm. They wouldn't have Mr. Gardiner as a master at the College here if there was anything wrong with him, now, would they?

  (MRS. TRAFFORD *folds ladder and leans it against wall above french windows, then fastens blouse cuffs.*)

MRS. TRAFFORD. Well, I hope you're right . . . Do you think you can manage now, Nannie?

  (MRS. TRAFFORD *crosses to above downstage crate, picks up coat and puts it on,* NANNIE *helping.*)

I don't want to be here when they arrive. Mr. Trafford's coming to fetch me.

NANNIE. Oh, what a shame. I was thinking you'd be here just to welcome them.

MRS. TRAFFORD. No. It's much better not.

  (*She starts to put on her things.*)

Did you get a chance to speak to him at all at the wedding?

NANNIE. Mr. Gardiner? Oh yes, 'm, I did. Only for a minute, though, of course. He come all across the room to speak to me. (*Crossing below sofa back to above trolley to finish laying places.*) I thought it was very nice of him.

MRS. TRAFFORD. Yes, he has good manners.

  (MRS. TRAFFORD *looks round for bag, crosses to sofa, takes bag from downstage corner, sits on arm: takes out compact.*)

NANNIE. Radiant she looked, driving off with him after the wedding. I said to Miss Capper at the time: of all the children I've ever looked after, I was fonder of Miss Rachel than any of them. And I'll tell you why. She has a loving heart.

MRS. TRAFFORD. Like her father.

NANNIE (*surprised*). Well, you couldn't have anyone nicer to take after.

MRS. TRAFFORD. It's not always safe to be quite so nice.

NANNIE (*puzzled*). Safe?

MRS. TRAFFORD. You nearly always have to pay for a generous impulse. Oh, I've seen it happen so often with Mr. Trafford. Over and over again in India. (*Rises, crosses to above upstage crate, picks up two books from floor and puts on shelves.*) I was always trying to persuade him not to be so friendly with Indians—not to have them to the house, or at least not to go to theirs. It didn't do, you know, in those days, for a Government official. And, of course, in the end, they let him down.

(*Sounds of arrival. Car door slams.*)

Ah, here is Mr. Trafford. Sure you can manage now, Nannie?

PAUL (*off*). All right, darling, I'll see to that.

(NANNIE *picks up tray from sofa, moves upstage.*)

NANNIE. Yes, 'm, thank you. (*Listening.*) Glory be to goodness! That's never them, is it?

(PAUL'S *voice can be heard in the hall.*)

PAUL (*off*). We'll have to alter that step. Everyone'll trip over it.

(NANNIE *crosses to* R. *of door.*)

NANNIE. Oh dear, oh dear, and I've not started the supper.

(*She meets* RACHEL *in the doorway.* RACHEL *looks tired and drawn, anything but radiant.*)

Well, here you are, dearie, welcome home!

RACHEL (*flatly*). Thank you, Nannie. (*She kisses her; then calls over her shoulder.*) Leave the bags, darling, we'll take them up after. (*Then, seeing* MRS. TRAFFORD, *tonelessly.*) Oh hullo, Mummy. (*Crosses to* MRS. TRAFFORD—L. *of her.*)

MRS. TRAFFORD. You've caught me. I didn't mean to be here. *How* are you, my darling?

RACHEL (*with a tired smile*). A bit battered. We racketed about rather.

MRS. TRAFFORD. I know! We were amazed to get a postcard from Naples. Whatever made you rush off down there?

RACHEL (*cutting her off sharply*). Here's Paul. (*Crosses* MRS. TRAFFORD *between crates to french windows.*)

(PAUL *comes in, looking through the letters he has found on the hall table. He, too, seems strained and preoccupied. He looks up and sees* MRS. TRAFFORD.)

PAUL. Oh. Good evening.

(*He hesitates. Then pulls himself together, goes over to* R. *of* MRS. TRAFFORD *and kisses her.*)

MRS. TRAFFORD. Well, it's lovely just to see you both.

PAUL (*with a bow*). Il piacere e di ambe le parti.

(MRS. TRAFFORD *looks blank.* RACHEL *laughs.*)

RACHEL. It's all right. He does this all the time. It only means the pleasure's mutual.

PAUL (*gives* MRS. TRAFFORD *a dazzling smile and turns* R. *upstage to* L. *of* NANNIE). How are you, Nannie? (*He shakes hands with her.*)

NANNIE. Very well, thank you, sir. Welcome home.

PAUL (*slightly taken aback*). Oh. Thank you.

NANNIE. You'll be wanting your supper. I meant to have it all ready for you. (*She goes out.*)

(PAUL *looks at* MRS. TRAFFORD. *He smiles and then crosses above sofa to above trolley, opening letter.*)

MRS. TRAFFORD (*crossing to* L. *of sofa*). Well, how are you both? Did you have a nice time?

(RACHEL *gives* PAUL *a quick look. He answers without looking up from his letter.*)

PAUL. The weather wasn't too good.

(*Pause.*)

RACHEL (*at french windows, noticing curtains*). We had those in Mandrapore: years ago.

(MRS. TRAFFORD *crosses above crates to french windows above* RACHEL.)

MRS. TRAFFORD. They were the best I could find.

RACHEL (*crossing between crates to* D.C.). Ah well, we'll soon get it all sorted out.

PAUL (*handing* RACHEL *a letter over back of sofa*). Sorry, darling, this is for you.

(RACHEL *crosses to* L.C. *of sofa, takes letter over back and sits on back.*)

RACHEL. Oh! From your mother. (*Looking at the envelope.*) "Mrs. P. A. Gardiner." It's no use. I don't recognise myself. (*Smiles at her mother and starts to read the letter.*)

(*Pause.*)

MRS. TRAFFORD (*feeling stranded*). You didn't stay very long in Venice.

RACHEL (*still reading*). No. No, we didn't.

(*Pause.*)

PAUL (*also reading*). Too cold. Everywhere in the north was too cold.

RACHEL (*puzzled*). She wants to give you another present.

PAUL (*sighing*). Oh! No.

RACHEL. She's found a Sheraton desk and do you want it.

PAUL (*turns away, frowning*). I shouldn't think so. Do you?

(*Pause.*)

RACHEL (*putting her hand to her forehead*). I'm still on a train . . . A train that rolls like a boat.

(*Pause.*)

(MRS. TRAFFORD *crosses* L.C. *by* L. *of upstage crate.*)

MRS. TRAFFORD (*feeling unwanted*). Well, I must be off. I don't know what's happened to Charles. He was supposed to be fetching me. You weren't meant to find me here, Paul. You mustn't start regretting you've in-laws who live in the district.

PAUL. If you hadn't lived here, I should never have met Rachel, should I?

MRS. TRAFFORD (*wishing he hadn't*). No.

(*Pause.*)

RACHEL (*smiling at her mother*). I shall stop moving soon.

(PAUL *opens another note.*)

PAUL. Oh blast! They've gone and changed my class-room.

(RACHEL *rises, turns to* PAUL *over back of sofa.*)

RACHEL. Rome was lovely, though, wasn't it, darling? We so wished we'd been there all the time.

PAUL. 'm. The weather cheered up a bit, too. (*He puts the letters in his pocket and crosses to door by above sofa.*) Well, I think I'll just go and get the things upstairs. (*To* MRS. TRAFFORD.) Don't go till I come back. We must have a drink. (*He goes out.*)

(MRS. TRAFFORD *moves in towards* RACHEL, *about to speak.* RACHEL *moves above sofa to fire.*)

RACHEL. Thank you so much for starting to cope with the house.

MRS. TRAFFORD (*to* U.L. *of sofa, urgently*). Rachel—tell me—is all well?

RACHEL (*with a sigh*). Oh, what do you expect?

MRS. TRAFFORD (*concerned*). Rachel . . . my darling . . .

RACHEL (*crossing to* U.R. *of sofa, quietly, looking at her*). Why did you have to do it? Why couldn't you have left the whole thing alone?

MRS. TRAFFORD. Darling, we *had* to know.

RACHEL (*angry*). He'd never have known at all if it hadn't been for you. It's the knowing that does the harm—not the thing itself. But we can't talk about it: we haven't talked about it at all.

MRS. TRAFFORD. We were only thinking of your happiness.

RACHEL (*wearily*). Oh, I suppose so.

MRS. TRAFFORD. *Paul* understood that. *He* thought it perfectly reasonable that your father and I should want to know all we could about his—well, about his background.

RACHEL. Of course he did. He's like that. He's far too conscientious about the whole thing, that's the trouble. He feels guilty. Don't you understand? He can't help feeling that perhaps he ought never to have married me.

MRS. TRAFFORD (*turns away slightly* L.). Well, my dear, of course, I must say that . . .

RACHEL. Oh, it's all very well for *you* to feel that, but when *he* does it's . . . it's paralysing. Italy was horrible.

(CHARLES TRAFFORD *comes in at the french window. He would have been a very distinguished civil servant if he hadn't always looked forward too eagerly to the day, five years ago now, when he would retire to the life of a bookish country gentleman. He crosses to between crates.*)

CHARLES. Hullo, Rachel.

RACHEL (*startled*). Daddy!

(RACHEL *crosses by* L. *of sofa and* R. *of* MRS. TRAFFORD *to* R. *of* CHARLES.)

CHARLES. You're early, aren't you ? Or am I late as usual?

MRS. TRAFFORD. You're late, Charles.

CHARLES. Oh. Sorry. (*He kisses* RACHEL *affectionately*.) Well, my dear, how was Italy? Did it come up to your expectations?

RACHEL (*trying to avoid his eyes*). Italy . . . well, we . . . It was rather cold, I . . . We didn't really . . . Oh . . .

(*She can't hold back her tears, and hurries from the room by* L. *of sofa and* R. *of* MRS. TRAFFORD—*leaving door open.* MRS. TRAFFORD *crosses up to shut door, moves down* C. *to* R. *of* CHARLES.)

MRS. TRAFFORD. Charles, she's dreadfully unhappy.

(*Pause.* CHARLES *remains very calm, perhaps to keep his wife calm. He crosses and sits* L. *side of upstage crate*—L. *of* MRS. TRAFFORD —*takes out pipe and pouch.*)

CHARLES. Oh! Have you any idea why?

MRS. TRAFFORD (*impatiently*). Oh, why do you suppose? It's come between them already.

CHARLES. Oh, for Heaven's sake, Nina, you didn't start talking about that as soon as you set eyes on her?

MRS. TRAFFORD. Of course not. I simply asked if all was well.

CHARLES (*looks at her quizzically*). I suppose it wasn't perfectly obvious what was in your mind?

MRS. TRAFFORD. No doubt it was obvious. It's in all our minds. All the time. It must be.

CHARLES. *It must not.* The only chance for their happiness is that we should put this thing right out of our minds—forget it altogether.
MRS. TRAFFORD. It's no use, Charles. It's too big to forget.
CHARLES. Well, is it, my dear? . . . I know it seems big, but after all, whatever his father may have done, it's nothing to do with the boy himself. *He's* not a murderer.
MRS. TRAFFORD. But he *is* the son of one. You can't get away from that. If his father was a duke you wouldn't forget it.
CHARLES (*amused, affectionate*). Poor old Nina. You're thinking of Charles Nottingham. I believe that's part of the trouble.
   (MRS. TRAFFORD *crosses to sit downstage arm of sofa.*)
MRS. TRAFFORD (*who enjoys seeing herself as a snob*). Well, there is something dreadfully lower-middle-class about murder. Those awful little houses where it happens . . . the stuffy, smelly lives of the witnesses . . . (*She shudders.*)
CHARLES. Well, I like him. Don't forget he was perfectly willing to release her. He left the decision entirely to *her.*
MRS. TRAFFORD. That was cruel. Don't tell me he didn't know what she'd do.
CHARLES. Well, at least she's gone into it with her eyes open, knowing, well, all there is to be known. There was no reason why she shouldn't if she chose.
MRS. TRAFFORD. It's no use, Charles . . . When he came in just now —I meant to be nice to him, I *was* nice to him—but I couldn't help feeling . . . (*Rises, crosses to* R. *of* CHARLES.) Oh, don't you see? It's inevitable. Besides, it's not only me. They find it between themselves . . .
   (PAUL *comes in* U.C., *shutting door.* MRS. TRAFFORD *crosses below sofa and trolley to* R. *of trolley.*)
CHARLES (*rises, crosses to* L. *of* PAUL, *shaking hands with him*). Well, Paul, how are you? I thought I must just stay and shake hands with you. Now we'll be off.
PAUL. You must have a drink before you go.
CHARLES (*putting a hand on his arm*). No, really, my boy, some other time.
PAUL. There won't be another time—quite like this.
   (*They look blank, disconcerted.* PAUL *takes out cigarette case.*)
You don't seem to realise how important you are. You're our first guests.

(*He hands cigarettes to* MRS. TRAFFORD—*over back of sofa downstage.*)

MRS. TRAFFORD (*crossing above trolley to take cigarette over back of sofa*). Oh . . . well . . . thank you.

(PAUL *crosses below* CHARLES *to downstage cupboard under bookcase* L. CHARLES *takes matches from pocket, lights cigarette over back of sofa.* PAUL *opens a cupboard and finds it empty.*)

PAUL. Oh, Lord! I hope there *is* something to drink—after all that.
(*They laugh.*)
I'm sure there ought to have been some sherry to come across from my old rooms. (PAUL *looks round—rises—crosses to box* R. *of downstage crate.*)

MRS. TRAFFORD (*above trolley—looking round*). I suppose this might be made into quite a pretty room.

(CHARLES *crosses to books* U.L.C.)

PAUL (*at crate; puts top box over on to box* R. *of it—looks in underneath box*). Not bad. I'd have liked something better for Rachel. But it'll be a nice change for me after five years in college.

(MRS. TRAFFORD *crosses down to table* D.R., *picks up a book, looks at its title and sighs.*)

MRS. TRAFFORD. . . . "The Structure of Choric Odes in Aeschylean Tragedy" . . . Oh dear—it terrifies me to have such a learned son-in-law.

(PAUL, *having found some sherry, rises, crosses to downstage cupboard, putting sherry on upstage crate.*)

PAUL. Ah, here we are. Good. At least, I hope it's good. Now for some glasses. I don't know where anything is yet.

CHARLES (*who has been wandering round, looking at the books* U.C. *to* U.R. *of* PAUL). It's appalling how one forgets . . . I doubt if I could read a word of Greek now . . .

(PAUL *gets sherry glasses out of cupboard—puts them on crate and stands* U.L. *of it.*)

PAUL. Quite soon no one'll be able to.

CHARLES. No one?

PAUL. Well, fewer and fewer boys learn it every year. The Classical Sixth here is dwindling fast. (*Takes out handkerchief.*)

CHARLES (*sighing*). Oh dear, oh dear.

MRS. TRAFFORD. Why does it matter?

PAUL (*smiling*). Unemployment of classical masters, for one thing. (*He starts cleaning the dusty glasses.*)
CHARLES (*crossing to back of sofa; downstage end*). Besides, my dear Nina, there's no better training for the growing mind than Latin and Greek.
PAUL (*interested and sceptical*). You really think that?
CHARLES. Don't you? (*Turns to* PAUL.)
PAUL. Oh well, I'm biased. I hope it's true.
CHARLES. I'm sure of it.

(MRS. TRAFFORD *puts books back on table, crosses from* D.R. *to sit on downstage arm of armchair* R.)

MRS. TRAFFORD. But why? That's what I never can make out. People who've had a classical education always say that. But they never explain why.

(PAUL *and* CHARLES *look at each other, stymied.*)

CHARLES. Go on. It's your job.
PAUL. I want to hear what you think.

(*Deadlock. They both laugh.* CHARLES *makes an effort.*)

CHARLES. Well, in the first place, Latin and Greek are extremely difficult. If you can master them, you can master most things . . .
PAUL (*crossing to* L. *of* CHARLES). Isn't it more a question of learning to be *asteios*—civilised? I mean, surely, there's really only one choice we ever have to make—in anything—not only in morals and politics—but in private life, in personal relations, even in matters of taste, amusement: are we to be Greeks or barbarians?
CHARLES (*enthusiastic*). Yes, yes, yes! That's it! (*Turning on* NINA.) And if we don't know the difference, we're barbarians!

(*They all laugh.*)

MRS. TRAFFORD. But everyone always forgets it all. You were supposed to be very good at Classics, weren't you, Charles, at Cambridge? Yet whenever I ask you to translate a Latin inscription in a church, or a motto on a crest or anything, you never can. (*Takes ashtray from* D.R. *table—puts on trolley.*)
CHARLES. It's perfectly true. I used to be quite good but now . . . I doubt if I could make out a word.

(CHARLES *picks up a book—the* Coephoroi—*from downstage pile by table* L.C., *moves to* U.R. *of* PAUL *and reads out a passage at random.*)

Iou, iou,
Cophois auto cai catheudousin mateen
Akranta badzo. Poi Clutaimneestra? Ti dra?

(PAUL *takes foil off sherry bottle.* CHARLES *starts to puzzle out the Greek.*)

Let me see—iou, iou, what's that? Just a cry, I suppose? a shout?

PAUL (*amused*). "Ho there within!" That's the sort of translation we schoolmasters like. Shakespearean! (PAUL *draws cork with corkscrew from his pocket.*)

CHARLES. *Cophois*—"blind", or "deaf", or something—*cai catheudousin*—"asleep". *Mateen* means "in vain", doesn't it? . . . Oh yes, I see —"I shout in vain. They must be deaf or sleeping". (PAUL *pours two glasses of sherry.*)

PAUL. Very good. Straight into blank verse! (*Up to door, open it—call off—shut door.*) Rachel! Come and have some sherry! (*Back to above crate, crosses* CHARLES.)

CHARLES (*excited, the feel of it coming back to him*). Wonderful stuff, . . . Greek tragedy . . . (*Goes on translating.*)

(PAUL *pours two more glasses of sherry.*)

"Where's Clytemnestra? What is she doing?" (*Then reads on.*)

Eoike nun autees epixeenou pelas
Aukeen peseithai pros dikeen pepleegmenos.

Eoike—"seems" . . . *Pelas*—"near" . . . Oh dear, I've forgotten everything. (PAUL *picks up two glasses and crosses* CHARLES *to* U.L. *of sofa.*) "It seems that her own neck is near the . . ." What's *epixeenou?*

PAUL (*turns, looks at him*). Block. Executioner's block.

(*Pause.*)

(PAUL *crosses to* U.L. *of* MRS. TRAFFORD. MRS. TRAFFORD *is frozen stiff with embarrassment.*)

CHARLES (*goes on translating*). "Why do you make all this clamour? What has happened?"

(PAUL *holds a drink out to* MRS. TRAFFORD.)

MRS. TRAFFORD. Oh . . . thank you. (*Rises, takes glass.*)

(PAUL *crosses above sofa to* R. *of* CHARLES.)

CHARLES. Ah, now I'm stuck again . . . I know all the words but . . .
(PAUL *hands* CHARLES *a sherry.*)

Oh, thanks. (PAUL *crosses to* R. *of upstage crate.*) Look, Paul—what's this next line mean? (CHARLES *crosses down to* R. *of* PAUL.)
> (*He shows the line to* PAUL, *who takes the book and reads the line under his breath.* MRS. TRAFFORD *sits in armchair.*)

PAUL. *Ton zonta kainein tous tethneekotas lego.* (*Then looks at* CHARLES *and says aloud.*) "I tell you the dead are murdering the living."
> (*Pause.* PAUL *shuts the book and throws it into box.* RACHEL *comes in. She has changed—not into the little frock we might expect but into elegant, casual clothes. She has recovered her poise and looks very beautiful. She crosses above sofa to above* MRS. TRAFFORD.
> PAUL *turns, picks up two glasses of sherry.*
> CHARLES *steps back to above upstage crate;* PAUL *crosses* CHARLES *to above sofa to* L. *of* RACHEL *and hands her the sherry.*)

RACHEL. Wonderful flowers in our room, Mummy. You shouldn't have bothered.

MRS. TRAFFORD. Paul, I can't think why on earth we took this sherry; we haven't time. We must be going.

CHARLES (*crossing to* L. *of sofa*). No, Nina, wait a bit—we must drink their health.

MRS. TRAFFORD (*stubs out cigarette*). Well, don't forget we've got to collect those plants on the way home.

CHARLES. I know, but it won't take a moment just to drink to them. (*To* RACHEL *and* PAUL.) Or is that being too conventional?

RACHEL (*smiling at him*). No—no—of course not, if you want to, darling.
> (RACHEL *and* PAUL *hold hands.*)

CHARLES. Well—I do—I do. Here's the greatest happiness to you both. (*Drinks.*)

MRS. TRAFFORD. Rachel—Paul! (*Drinks.*)

RACHEL. Thank you, darling.
> (MRS. TRAFFORD *puts glass on trolley, rises, crosses below* RACHEL *and* PAUL *to door.* CHARLES *drains glass.*)

MRS. TRAFFORD. Now, come along, Charles—do.
> (*At the door.*)

Good-bye, Paul. (PAUL *moves slightly forward.*) Don't bother to come out.

PAUL. Right. See you again soon.
> (RACHEL *crosses* PAUL *to door.* MRS. TRAFFORD *goes out, followed by* RACHEL.

CHARLES *puts glass on table* D.L.C., *crosses up into doorway*—L. *of* PAUL.)

CHARLES. Well, thank you for the drink, Paul. You know I . . . I really am very glad about you and Rachel. No reservations about that.

PAUL (*looks at him*). Thank you very much, sir.

CHARLES. Good-bye.

(CHARLES *goes out.* PAUL *crosses above and by* R. *of sofa to below it, then to* R. *of upstage crate—puts glass on it, turns, looks at* Aeschylus. *He crosses down to above box, picks up book, finds place—reads line, shuts book and throws it back into box. Then he crosses between crates to shut french windows.*)

PAUL (*hardly more than a sigh*). Oh God . . .

(RACHEL *comes back, shuts door and crosses* D.C. *to* R. *of crates.*)

RACHEL. Well, that's over. (*Crosses to between crates.*) I haven't seen you for ages, darling. How are you?

PAUL (*going to her*). Very well, thank you. How are you? (*He kisses her. They laugh.*) I feel like that, too. When we've been with other people for a few minutes.

(RACHEL *crosses below sofa and flings herself down on it, head* D.S., *with a sigh of relief and relaxation.*)

RACHEL. Oh, this is wonderful . . . we're home! Do you realise that, darling? Home!

PAUL. Yes. (*He wanders away and looks at some books.*) It won't do, you know. (RACHEL *stiffens, tense again.*) Having them so near. It'll never never work.

RACHEL. But . . . (*Turns downstage, sits in corner of sofa.*) I thought he was being so nice.

PAUL. They both were. Straining every nerve to put me at my ease. The atmosphere was thick with tact.

RACHEL. Well, darling, what else can people do? You wouldn't like it if they didn't.

PAUL (*smiling*). The nicer people are on these occasions, the more aware one is of *why* they are being nice. The few minutes they were here, no one was thinking of anything else.

(*He turns away,* L. RACHEL *watches him anxiously. He speaks with savage irony.*)

If there'd been a freshly killed corpse in the room we could hardly have been more chatty and unperturbed.

(*Pause. Then he turns to her with a smile.*)

Sorry, darling. I'd be all right, if I didn't love you.

(*He smiles at her again. She looks at him in silence.*)

If this hadn't been all mixed up with our getting married, I don't suppose I'd have turned a hair. At any other time, I'd have taken it more or less in my stride. But just now—when it matters, more than ever before, what one . . . what one is . . . it's no time to be riddled with self-doubt . . .

RACHEL. Don't you give *me* credit for any judgment?

PAUL. No, none. (*Crosses, kneels* L. *of sofa.*) Saints don't look after number one. They land on racks. (PAUL *kisses* RACHEL *over back of sofa.*)

RACHEL. You under-estimate me, darling. I'm extremely shrewd. After all, I've had plenty of other offers. I think you're a splendid proposition.

PAUL. Your family don't.

RACHEL. I always wish you'd never told them.

PAUL. I couldn't have done that.

RACHEL. If I didn't mind, what's it got to do with anyone else? It's not their business.

(PAUL *rises, crosses to* R. *of upstage crate with back to* RACHEL.)

PAUL. If they cared tuppence for your welfare, once they knew I was adopted, of course they'd want to know my history—medically, if nothing else. Look at the Carter boy—both parents chronic alcoholics, mother committed suicide—look what happened to him . . .

RACHEL (*laughing*). Well, darling, he was schizophrenic . . .

(PAUL *looks at her.* RACHEL's *laughter ceases.* NANNIE *comes in with the soup on a tray. She crosses above sofa to above trolley and transfers soup to trolley.*)

NANNIE. Here you are. Nice hot soup to be going on with.

(*Silence.* PAUL *and* RACHEL *are visibly not at ease.*)

RACHEL (*sniffing the soup*). Mushroom. Delicious.

NANNIE. Och, sure it's only out of an old tin can. Still, there you are.

(NANNIE *puts tray in armchair, pulls armchair round at right-angles to sofa, moves standard lamp to beside armchair, switches on.* PAUL *takes cork off corkscrew, puts corkscrew in pocket, drains sherry glass, pours himself another glass and drinks.*)

Oh, I was nearly forgetting. Your mother rang up, sir, tea-time—Mrs. Gardiner, I should say.

PAUL (*impatient*). Oh! What did she want?

NANNIE. Just to welcome you, sir, that's all. She said it'd be too late to ring when she got in this evening, so to give her love and best wishes to both of you. (NANNIE *picks up* MRS. TRAFFORD'S *sherry glass from trolley, tray from armchair, crosses above armchair and sofa to door*.)

PAUL. I see. Thank you.

(NANNIE *glances from one to the other of them and goes out*.)
(PAUL *picks up sherry bottle*.)

More sherry?

RACHEL. No, thank you.

(PAUL *replaces bottle on crate*.)

It's no use, darling. I find this so exciting . . . This is the real beginning. Not Venice, not hotels and restaurant meals, but this . . . tinned soup by an electric fire.

(PAUL *crosses below sofa, sits downstage of* RACHEL *and kisses her*.)

PAUL. I love you—I love you—I love you. You're good (*Kiss.*) and beautiful (*Kiss.*) and kind (*Kiss.*) . . . And I'm odious. I'm an insufferable, introverted, anxiety-ridden fuss-pot. Bully me, darling, shut me up. (*Kiss.*) Only consent, if you can, to bear the intolerable burden . . . of having me about the place. (*Kiss.*)

RACHEL. Eat your soup, darling, while it's hot. (*Pushes* PAUL *up*. PAUL *rises, crosses below trolley to sit in armchair*.)

PAUL. Yes, yes, you see . . . ? You're perfect! That was the only possible answer to give! How did you know?

RACHEL. Simple peasant wisdom—picked it up in the Land Army.

PAUL. I can't quite see you as a Land Girl.

RACHEL. I never could see myself. For two years I hardly looked in a mirror.

(*They laugh and settle down to eat.* RACHEL *takes her bowl and tucks up her feet on the sofa. They eat for a moment in silence. They are happy.*)

RACHEL (*looking round*). I think I'm actually going to like this room.

PAUL (*also looking round*). 'm. The Snot used to have it. I used to come here for confirmation classes.

RACHEL. What repulsive names you gave them!

PAUL. He'd been a naval chaplain. He was always talking about snotties . . . I used to sit there (*Points to* D.C.) and ask awkward questions. I was the boy with doubts.

RACHEL. I'm sure you were. You're King Doubt.

PAUL. The Snot used to love it. They always like it, up to a point . . . provided you come to the right conclusions. It's called "thinking for yourself".

RACHEL. I suppose this room must seem quite different to you . . . All these schoolboy associations . . . I hope they don't spoil it for you.

PAUL. On the contrary, they make a tradition. I suppose, having no family tradition of my own . . .

RACHEL. I loathe family traditions. One of ours is not smoking between courses . . . Give me a cigarette.

(PAUL *takes out cigarette case and offers it to* RACHEL. *She takes a cigarette.* PAUL *lights it with lighter from his pocket.*)

PAUL. All the same, you know, I dare say that is partly why I came back here as a master. You know how people in the war used to get sudden whiffs of their childhood—most people got their homes, of course. I used to get this place . . . Autumn evenings in Great Court, cricket on summer afternoons . . . Odd. I'm not really an old-school character. I didn't particularly like the place. But at least I felt more at home here than I did at home . . .

RACHEL. Oh, I got that wrong then. I thought she did manage to make you feel it was your home.

PAUL. Up to the age of nine. Not once she'd told me I was adopted. After that, if she sent me away from a meal to wash my hands, I used to feel—"There, that's it—I belong to a different world, a dirty-fingered world . . ."

RACHEL (*laughing*). I'm sure you always seemed utterly self-possessed.

PAUL. Oh, I dare say. That's a trick that's soon learnt. Shall we have some wine?

RACHEL. Have we got any?

(PAUL *rises, crosses below trolley and sofa to crate.*)

PAUL. There's a bottle or two of schoolmasters' hock in the crate.

RACHEL. All right—let's.

(PAUL *goes to get wine from crate.*)

PAUL. Nowadays, of course, you're supposed to tell children they're adopted before they're three; less of a shock. There's even a recommended method of approach . . . "Ordinary mummies have to take what they can get, but (*Takes out bottle of hock.*) I *chose* you out of a whole bunch of little boys and girls because I liked you best!" (*Taking foil off bottle.*) In those days they hadn't got it quite so taped. She did it very well. She was kind . . . gentle . . . tactful. That was the first time I resented tact.

RACHEL. It can't have been easy for her.

PAUL (*takes corkscrew from pocket*). No. I can't remember what she said. I only remember she seemed to change as she said it. You're not my mother, I thought, you're not my mother. I've been had. The whole thing's a swiz! (*Draws cork.*)

RACHEL (*laughing delightedly at his expression*). Yes! Yes! You must have looked just like that!

(PAUL, *holding bottle, crosses above upstage crate to cupboard and gets two hock glasses.*)

PAUL. What do you mean?

RACHEL (*seriously, seeing the little boy in him*). Nine and outraged . . .

(PAUL *crosses above sofa to above trolley, puts glasses down—pours hock; puts bottle on floor* R. *of armchair.*)

PAUL (*laughs*). Anyway, after that I never felt it safe to take anything for granted: certainly nothing about her. She was always awfully good to me, you know—I had everything . . . but it was all suspect. I used to sit opposite her at meals and think—I shall never know what you really feel.

RACHEL (*laughing*). Poor woman . . .! Darling, you don't make it easy for people, do you?

PAUL (*hands* RACHEL *hock*). Oh, I know. I'm not justifying it. I'm simply explaining how it happened. (*Takes own glass.*) From then on, I never felt quite at home in the world.

RACHEL. Till now?

PAUL (*looking into her eyes*). Till now. Yes. (*Puts glass down, crosses above sofa to bookshelves, takes fifty-cigarette box, puts it on upstage crate, while he fills his cigarette case from the box.* RACHEL *puts soup-cup on trolley.*) And now this other damned thing has to crop up . . . Oh hell, why can't things ever be simple? (*Pause.*) One doesn't ask much. Only to be able to take oneself for granted.

RACHEL (*very quietly*). I love you . . .

(PAUL *turns, looks at her across the room and smiles.* NANNIE *comes in with the second course. She crosses to table* U.L.C. *above bookshelves: tray on table.*)

NANNIE. Here you are. I've done you croquettes.
> (*She puts down the tray and knocks over a pile of books.*)

Oh! Books, books, books! I've never seen so many books. (NANNIE *takes casserole and two plates from tray, crosses above sofa to above trolley.*) I was saying to Mrs. Trafford just now, there's no doubt about Mr. Gardiner being clever, anyway.

PAUL (*joking*). Perhaps there was doubt about my being good?
> (NANNIE *puts casserole and plates down, takes soup-cups and spoons.*)

NANNIE (*to* RACHEL). Sharp, isn't he? No, sir, of course there wasn't. Not in my mind anyway.

PAUL. But Mrs. Trafford wasn't so sure?
> (NANNIE *crosses above sofa to* L.C., U.R. *of* PAUL. PAUL *taking corkscrew from cork: corkscrew into pocket.*)

NANNIE. Well, you know what mothers are, sir. Always thinking some harm's going to come to their precious children . . .

RACHEL (*sits up, legs off sofa, cutting her short*). Nannie, could we have some salt?

NANNIE. There you are, dear. On the tray. (RACHEL *shrugs, leans over, takes ashtray from* U.R. *corner of trolley, stubs out cigarette.*) I told her, I said, it doesn't matter *who* a person is or *what* a person is, so long as he's fond of you . . .

RACHEL. All right, Nannie, that'll do.
> (NANNIE *crosses* U.L.C.—*puts cups on tray, picks up tray, crosses to door.*)

NANNIE. Oh dear, yes, I mustn't stand here gossiping. Ring if you want anything, won't you?
> (RACHEL *takes lid off casserole and starts serving.*)

RACHEL. I don't think we shall want any more. What about you, darling?

PAUL. Coffee, perhaps?

NANNIE. It's all ready. (*She goes out, shutting door.*)

PAUL (*crossing above sofa to armchair*). I think she knows.

RACHEL. Nannie? Of course not.

PAUL. What was all that about then? (*Sits armchair.*)

RACHEL. That's just Nannyism. (*Puts* PAUL'S *plate down—indicates croquettes.*) You try a croquette.
> (RACHEL *serves own meal.*)

PAUL. 'm . . . Not bad! Clever old thing. You said she wouldn't be able to cook anything but bread and milk.

(RACHEL *says nothing but picks up lid of casserole—sits gazing at it.* PAUL *glances at her. He refills hock glasses.*)

What is it, darling?

(RACHEL *replaces lid on casserole, takes plate and curls up in upstage corner of sofa.*)

RACHEL. I was just thinking about your mother. Strange of her to write to *me*!

PAUL. She and I don't find it easy to communicate these days. I think we both feel a bit guilty.

RACHEL. I don't wonder she does—it was astonishing of her to tell you that.

PAUL. I drove her to it. I was awful to her.

RACHEL. But she *must* have foreseen that you might come in one day and say "Look, I must know! Who am I?"—especially if you were going to get married . . .

PAUL. Yes—but she couldn't have foreseen the other things I said. I've never really told you. I said that she'd taken me up as a hobby because her own love-life had gone wrong. I said I'd been nothing all my life but a guinea-pig for a rich woman's experiments in artificial domestic affection . . . That's when she lost her temper. I'd never seen her really angry before. " Very well, then," she said, "I'll tell you. Your father was hanged!"

(*Pause.* PAUL *gives a little laugh.*)

That was rather more than I'd bargained for. Then you all arrived for lunch and somehow we've never been able to continue that conversation.

RACHEL. All through that lunch you looked ghastly.

PAUL. Your mother kept talking about lampshades. I couldn't fix my attention on what she was saying. At one point I was quite light-headed.

RACHEL. Actually she thought you had 'flu. She was afraid of catching it.

(*They both laugh.*)

PAUL (*refills wine glasses*). She'd started talking about upper-class pronunciations—lawndry and larndry, gurls and gairls—and I thought: "What would she *do*, if I said, 'Oh, by the way, I do hope you've no objection: it seems I'm the son of a murderer'." (*Replaces bottle on floor.*)

(*Again they both laugh.* NANNIE *comes in and crosses* L. *of sofa with the coffee. The laughter ceases abruptly.*)

NANNIE. Here you are, then. Here's your coffee.

RACHEL. Thank you, Nannie. (*Points to table upstage of bookshelves.*) Just leave it there, will you?

(NANNIE *puts coffee on table and crosses to door.*)

NANNIE. Supper all right?

RACHEL. Delicious, thank you.

(NANNIE *goes out, shutting door.*)

PAUL. Do you think she heard?

(RACHEL *sits up, swinging feet off sofa, puts plate on trolley.*)

RACHEL. No. Anyway she wouldn't realise it was serious.

PAUL (*sighing*). Oh, what a curse the whole thing is . . . It seeps into everything like a fog. Like a bad smell. And to have landed you in it . . .

RACHEL (*half mocking*). Darling, darling, darling . . . I *cannot* spend the whole of my life telling you I—do—not—mind.

PAUL (*looking at her*). That's what I loathe . . . Knowing there must always be something about me that you have "not to mind"—to put up with—to swallow.

RACHEL (*laughing*). You're determined neither to eat your cake nor have it!

PAUL. Oh darling, you are wonderful! You always laugh at the right moment . . . just like that day . . . after lunch when I told you. No one else would have laughed. It saved me, I think. Why did you?

RACHEL (*laughing again*). Darling, the relief . . . You looked so tragic, I'd made sure it was bad news.

PAUL (*glumly*). Wasn't it?

RACHEL To me—just then—there was only one kind of bad news. There still is.

(NANNIE *comes in to* R. *of door, closing door behind her.*)

NANNIE. There's a gentleman to see you, sir.

PAUL (*suddenly nervous*). A gentleman? What gentleman?

NANNIE. I fancy he's one of the masters at the college, sir. A Mr. Lamb.

PAUL (*jumping up, delighted*). The Lamb! Of course! Where is he?

Bring him in. (PAUL *rises, pushes trolley downstage, crosses to above sofa.* NANNIE *opens door and stands* L. *of it.* RACHEL *rises to above armchair.*)
    (*As* NANNIE *opens door,* ARTHUR LAMB *enters by* R. *of* NANNIE *to* L. *of* PAUL. *He is an elderly man of letters manqué—a considerable scholar, absent-minded, eccentric, charming.*)

LAMB. You sounded pleased, dear boy. How delightful! The rewards of eavesdropping . . . (*Then, seeing the napkin in* PAUL'S *hand.*) Oh dear, you're at table! I *am* sorry. I'll go at once. (*He turns to go.*)
    (RACHEL *moves in a step.* NANNIE *goes out, shutting door.*)

RACHEL (*laughing*). No, no. Stay—please . . . We'll be having coffee in a minute.
                (PAUL *turns to* RACHEL.)

PAUL. You know Rachel, don't you?

LAMB. Yes, yes of course, we met at the wedding. (*He bows to her.*) Besides, I know your distinguished father quite well.

PAUL. Have a glass of wine?

LAMB. No, thank you. Do go on with your meal, please. Don't let me interrupt.

PAUL. Well, sit down then.

LAMB. Very well, just for a moment. (*To* RACHEL.) Are you . . .?

RACHEL. No—no, I've finished.
    (LAMB *sits upstage corner of sofa.* PAUL *goes back to his place and goes on eating.* RACHEL *crosses above sofa to below table* L.C.—*starts pouring coffee.*)

LAMB. I looked in to pay you and your dear wife a belated call of welcome. I ought to have been here ages ago. Very remiss of me.

PAUL. We only got back this evening.

LAMB (*jumping up, horrified*). From your honeymoon? Oh, good gracious, you won't want me, then. I *am* sorry. Oh dear, I *am* sorry . . .
    (*He goes to the door and meets* NANNIE *coming in with a cup and saucer. She crosses to* R. *of* RACHEL *and gives them to her.*)

NANNIE. I thought you'd be wanting another cup.

RACHEL (*laughing*). Thank you, Nannie. Now you *must* stay.
                (NANNIE *goes out.*)

LAMB. No, no, really.

RACHEL. White?

LAMB (*giving in*). Oh, very well, then. (*Crosses to* C., R. *of* RACHEL.) No, black. I always drink my coffee black. To try and persuade myself I'm a man of the world. Ours is a dreadful profession, you know. One's always ashamed of it.

PAUL (*still eating*). You needn't be.

LAMB. I sometimes think: "No, no, no. Let it not be true. I am not—I cannot be—one of them". And yet I am, of course. There's no getting away from it. I am.

  (RACHEL *hands* LAMB *his coffee, and then crosses him, holding* PAUL's *coffee. She indicates upstage corner of sofa.* LAMB *crosses and sits.* RACHEL *hands* PAUL *his coffee.*)

RACHEL. Come and sit over here by Paul.

LAMB. Oh, thank you, thank you. Of course, you know what's wrong with them, my dear? So many of them are bachelors. Enemies to life. Oh, they swill their beer and tell their smoking-room stories. But underneath, they're dangerous—they're prim.

RACHEL (*to* PAUL *as she goes to coffee tray*). What a good thing I married you, darling.

LAMB. Since my dear wife died, I've come to realise more and more how much I owed to her. One needs to escape from that dreadful common-room atmosphere. It's not easy to preserve one's humanity in a public school.

PAUL. People like you and Mallory seem to manage it.

LAMB (*sighing*). Yes. Poor Mallory.

PAUL (*turning sharply*). What?

LAMB. Oh, of course, you've been away. You won't have heard . . .

PAUL. But what is it? What's happened?

  (RACHEL *crosses* D.C., L. *of sofa—with coffee cup.*)

LAMB. I'm afraid he's dreadfully ill.

PAUL. Ill?

LAMB. He went into hospital the week before last for observation. Now they say there's very little hope.

    (*Pause.*)

Tumour on the brain. Inoperable.

    (*Long pause.* PAUL *is moved.*)

PAUL. I suppose I owe more to him than to any living man . . . The two years I spent in his form changed the world for me.

LAMB (*eagerly*). I'm so glad to hear you say that. Of course, he's far and away the best man they've ever had here. He's made the Classical Sixth into something unique.

  (RACHEL *crosses* U.C. *to above sofa.*)

PAUL. I don't know how he did it. Looking back, now, it seems as if all the values of civilisation, of the human spirit, used to be—distilled in that shabby room . . . Oh, he didn't *do* it, really, I suppose. It was simply the—quality of his mind . . .
RACHEL. I thought they could operate nowadays for tumour on the brain? (*Sits L. arm of* PAUL's *chair*.)
LAMB. In this case, it seems—no.
RACHEL. He always seemed to me remote . . . cold . . .
PAUL. But you should have heard him taking his form. That flat, cold voice . . . He used to sound almost bored. But as you listened—some dull, difficult notion gradually became clear, precise, intelligible—quite casually, by an inflection of the voice, an edge of irony—he could set light in you a lasting passion for an idea . . . If I felt I could ever do for even one boy what he did for me, it would be worth the hell of being a schoolmaster.
LAMB. Well, but, my dear boy, you can, I'm sure. I've no doubt you do, every day. You're one of the very few of us here who have something of that quality.
PAUL. Mallory's form and your library . . . I suppose they were the two greatest benefits of my time here.
LAMB (*pleased*). Yes, you used the library a lot, didn't you? I remember you quite distinctly. I fancy you were there quite often when you should have been doing something else—physical training or something. I was quite aware of that, you know.

(RACHEL *rises, crosses above sofa to coffee tray, puts own cup down, picks up coffee pot.*)

PAUL. You never said anything.
LAMB. Well . . . I've always wanted the library to be a kind of refuge—a sanctuary—among other things. (RACHEL *crosses to L. of sofa, pours more coffee for* LAMB *over back of sofa. He turns to* RACHEL.) Do you know, when I took over the library, nearly forty years ago now, there were only a few hundred books—and nobody ever used it? Now we've got over twenty-seven thousand and nearly all in circulation.
RACHEL (*crosses above sofa to refill* PAUL's *cup*). But that's magnificent! And it's something that'll always be there, something permanent.
LAMB. Ah well, I don't know. Libraries die, like everything else.
RACHEL. Die?
LAMB. Look at the great libraries in our country houses—dead for

years, before they're finally broken up and sold . . . It worries me who's to take over the library when I go.

RACHEL (*sits* L. *arm of* PAUL's *chair, holding coffee pot*). Are you thinking of retiring?

LAMB. Well, no, my dear. I'm thinking of dying. I'm over seventy, you know. I'm only here at half-cock, so to speak. Stop-gap teaching, and—the library . . . And when I'm at luncheon in the Common Room and look down the table at our revered colleagues, I think to myself, "No, no, not a librarian amongst you. Scoutmasters, all of you! Hearty, narrow-minded men . . ." Except you, my boy. I have sometimes hoped you might consider taking on the library, when I'm gone.

PAUL. Me? Well, I don't know . . .

LAMB. You're the only man on the staff here with enough true humanity to make a good librarian. When some dirty little junior boy comes along—you know, one of those frost-bitten, chilblainy boys with bad circulations—children of elderly parents, I often think—and wants, say, an engineering text-book . . . It needs a man who can see that here may be the beginning of some great mechanical or scientific achievement. In our job we must be friends to life—even in its—its most unprepossessing forms . . . When some fat, pasty-faced fellow wants nothing but erotic poetry—give it to him, give it to him! A good librarian ought to be able to see that here may be—oh, not only a scholar in the making but perhaps a great specialist in nervous disorders—or—or a bishop. You have that imagination, my boy. You can see beyond your nose.

PAUL. I don't always like what I see.

LAMB. Ah well, no. That's what the chaplain would call our cross. . . . (*Puts coffee-cup on trolley—rises to go.* RACHEL *rises to above armchair.* PAUL *rises to below armchair.* LAMB *crosses to* L. *of* RACHEL.) Good night, my dear girl. Forgive me for intruding. I remember how annoyed my dear wife used to be—in the early days—if someone interrupted our evenings together . . . Yes . . . How life slips through one's fingers! I came here for a term, you know, and I've stayed forty years. My whole life has been more or less . . . an accident, as it were. (*Shakes hands with* RACHEL.) Well, I hope for you this will be the first of many happy evenings—interrupted as seldom as possible by—by—garrulous old men. (*He turns to go and bumps into* NANNIE *in the doorway.*)

(RACHEL *moves down to put coffee-pot on trolley.*)
Oh, I beg your pardon—I beg your pardon.
NANNIE. Not at all, sir—not at all.
PAUL (*crossing by* R. *of and above armchair to door*). I'll come and see you out.
> (*They go out together.* NANNIE *shuts door; then crosses to table* L.C. *for coffee tray.*)

NANNIE. Funny old gentleman that. Eccentric.
> (RACHEL *stacks large plates, small plates, folds one napkin.*)

RACHEL. Nice though.
> (NANNIE *crosses above sofa to* L. *of trolley, puts coffee tray on sofa.*)

NANNIE. Still, you don't want people butting in like that. Oh dear, I can't get used to it somehow.
RACHEL. Used to what?
> (NANNIE *puts coffee-cup, milk and sugar from tray on to trolley.*)

NANNIE. Seems only the other day you were sitting by the nursery fire in your red dressing-gown, having your bread and milk. Now you're grown up, married, facing all the horrors of life . . .
RACHEL (*laughing*). Nannie . . . really . . .
NANNIE. Well, dear, you never know. (*Folds* RACHEL'S *napkin and puts it into ring.*) Your mother and I was talking about it only this evening . . . Marriage is a gamble at the best of times, but I told her—I said—Mr. Gardiner's all right, whatever his parents may have been. (*Picks up tray, about to push trolley.*)
RACHEL (*horrified, rounding on her*). You mean to say she told you? Oh, how could she? (*Throws napkin on table—sits armchair.*)
NANNIE. There, now, love, you don't mind *me* knowing, do you?
RACHEL (*frantic*). We don't want *anyone* to know . . . Oh, I suppose *I* don't mind so much, but Paul does. Naturally.
NANNIE. You know you can trust me. I won't mention a word. Not to a living soul. He needn't ever know that I know. (*Pushes trolley below sofa to* L. *of it, moving towards door.*)
RACHEL. Oh, how detestable! Why will people interfere?
NANNIE. Oh dear, I *am* sorry. I didn't know you'd mind so much . . .
> (*Crosses up to door pushing trolley.* PAUL *comes back and holds door open for her, then crosses to above sofa.*)

PAUL. We'll be seeing a lot of him, I expect. His house backs on our garden.

RACHEL. I shan't mind. He's nice.
NANNIE. Well, I'll be off to bed as soon as I've finished.
RACHEL (*preoccupied*). Yes, Nannie, good night. You mustn't tire yourself.
NANNIE. Good night, sir. (*Turning back to* L. *of* PAUL.) I'm . . . real glad about you and Miss Rachel. I am indeed, sir.
PAUL (*surprised, suspicious*). Oh, thank you. That's very kind. Good night.
    (NANNIE *pushes trolley out, shuts door behind her.*)
There it was again. Did you notice?
RACHEL (*deliberately casual*). Notice what, darling?
PAUL. The way she looked at me. A sort of . . . over-acted sympathy.
RACHEL (*rises to below armchair. Angrily, her nerve snapping*). Oh, don't keep on about it! It's such a bore!
    (*Pause.*)
PAUL (*clipped, defensive, supercilious*). I'm sorry. The last thing I want to do is to bore you.
    (*Pause. After a moment* PAUL *becomes aware she is crying.* (*He crosses below armchair and above* RACHEL *to* R. *of her.*)
Oh my darling . . . Don't . . . don't . . . What's wrong? Tell me.
RACHEL (*in tears*). We're—we're quarrelling.
PAUL. We're not, we're not. I'm sorry I spoke like that.
RACHEL. No, no, it was me. It was what I said. Of course you're not a bore. It's only that . . . it gets on my nerves . . . I suppose I'm tired, that's all.
PAUL. You're right. I ought to keep these dreary anxieties to myself.
RACHEL. It's all imagination, you know.
PAUL. Is it? Perhaps . . . I don't know, though. That look in her eyes . . . Did I imagine that?
RACHEL. I think so, yes. (*Crosses to sofa, sits downstage corner.*) Anyway, it's absurd to read all that into it. How can you ever be sure what a look in the eyes means?
PAUL (*crosses, kneels* R. *of* RACHEL, *facing her. Takes her in his arms*). I know what your eyes mean, my darling.
RACHEL. Do you?
PAUL (*looking into her eyes*). Quite, quite certainly. Without the shadow of a doubt . . . They're the most direct, the most honest

eyes I've ever seen . . . I'd trust your eyes always . . . I'd trust my whole life to your eyes . . .

(*She can't face him and turns away,* D.S., *weeping.*)

My darling . . . what's the matter?

RACHEL (*turns to look at* PAUL). I'm lying to you. You didn't imagine it. She does know.

(*Slight pause.*)

PAUL (*sits back on heels. Very angry, but quiet*). Oh my God! Why can't people keep their mouths shut?

RACHEL. *She* will. She's completely reliable. She promised.

PAUL. I suppose your mother told her?

RACHEL. I'm afraid so.

PAUL. Well, that's that. (*Rises, crosses below sofa to* D.C., R. *of crates.*) We shall have to leave here, that's all.

RACHEL. Surely it'd be better if Nannie left?

PAUL (*turns upstage*). What use is that? Your mother might find another *confidante*. (*Crosses* U.C.) Discretion doesn't seem her strong point.

RACHEL (*turns to watch him*). Would it matter so very much if people did get to know?

PAUL (*crosses* D.C.). I should lose my job, of course.

RACHEL (*rises, steps back*). But why? Why should you?

PAUL (*crosses* U.C.). I should think they'd give me a house at once, on the strength of it. Crippen's, don't you think it'd be called? My study would be known as the condemned cell—the drop—yes, that's it. (*Crosses* D.C., R. *of crates.*) If I sent for a boy to see me, it'd be known as "taking the drop".

RACHEL (*horrified by the bitterness, very quietly*). Paul, darling, don't.

(PAUL *feels in his pockets for his pipe.*)

PAUL. You've advised me often enough to take it lightly, make a joke of it. Well, that's the form the joke will take.

RACHEL. Your pipe's upstairs on the dressing-table.

PAUL. Is it? (*Crosses to door by* L. *of sofa—opens door.*) Oh, thanks.

RACHEL. Paul. (*Crosses between sofa and armchair to* D.R. *of door.*) We can't go on like this . . .

PAUL (*turns*). I couldn't agree more.

(*He goes out leaving door open.* RACHEL, *in despair, sits in armchair thinking.* NANNIE *puts her head round the door.*)

NANNIE. Ah! That's right! I thought I heard him go upstairs. (*She comes in and shuts the door. She crosses above sofa to* L. *of* RACHEL *between sofa and armchair*.) Now listen, dear, you're quite safe with me. And don't you *worry* so much. My nephew, Len—at least I call him my nephew—he couldn't have been a better son to Carrie, not if he was her own. And he's just the same—he's illegitimate, too.

RACHEL (*dazed*). Illegitimate? But Paul's . . . Is *that* what Mummy told you?

NANNIE (*not wanting to cause trouble*). Well, not in so many words, of course. She just said he was adopted: but from the way she spoke, I could put two and two together . . .

RACHEL (*realising what's happened, half laughing, half crying with relief*). Of course, of course. Oh dear, how absurd! Dear Nannie!

(PAUL *comes back, crossing* D.C. *by* L. *of sofa, filling pipe*.)

NANNIE (*crossing to above sofa*). Oh, there you are, sir! I just came in to ask about breakfast. D'you like corn flakes?

RACHEL. Just put them on the table, will you, Nannie? We'll have them if we want them. Good night.

NANNIE. Good night. Good night, sir. (*Goes out, shutting door*.)

RACHEL. Darling, it's all right! It's all right! She doesn't know a thing! It's too absurd! Mummy told her you were adopted, that's all. And she thought you were illegitimate!

PAUL (*quietly*). It's not quite the point, is it—whether other people know? The point is that *we don't*.

RACHEL (*puzzled*). What do you mean?

PAUL (*turning on her passionately, but with all defensive irony now dropped. This is what really worries him*). We've been told so little—the mere, bare fact! My mind can't leave it alone—probing, guessing, wondering—what *kind* of man was he? (*Moving up and down stage* L.) There are so many *kinds* of murder . . . calculated, callous murders for money, slow, cruel poisonings . . . savage, brutal attacks from rage or fear . . . sexual murders, insane murders . . . Oh, I suppose there are even a few respectable murders you could sympathise with . . . But not to know . . . ! Not to know the details—when it's the details that count . . . It was outrageous of her not to tell me more . . .

RACHEL. But she doesn't know any more.

PAUL (*turns to* RACHEL. *of sofa*). You believe that?

RACHEL. Either that or she'd promised never to say. They always . . . try to sever all connection, don't—they? . . . To give the child every chance.

PAUL (*turns away* L.). Every chance . . . Every chance to imagine freely . . . what seeds of violence and filth he carries in him . . .

RACHEL (*rises, crosses below sofa to* R. *of* PAUL). Need you think about that? I never do.

PAUL (*gripping her arms, fiercely*). *Can* you say that? Can you honestly say that it's never crossed your mind—even for a moment—what *is* he like? What has he in him? Cruelty, perhaps? Vice? Madness?

RACHEL. No, no, no. You haven't, you haven't.

(PAUL *crosses below upstage crate with back to* RACHEL.)

PAUL. That first evening in Venice, when I lost my temper with that American? Didn't you wonder then?

RACHEL (*steps downstage towards him, laughing*). Darling, no! I thought I'd be blasted out of existence! So did he, poor man! It was like a lightning flash, I didn't have time to wonder anything.

PAUL (*quietly*). I did. That's what this thing does. One begins to wonder what one's own feelings and actions mean . . . I no longer know what I am. I've become a stranger to myself.

(RACHEL *goes to him, taking him in her arms.*)

But not to me. You're not a stranger to me.

PAUL. Yes . . . I'm that, too.

RACHEL (*sharply*). No! *Not* to me. I love you. I know what you are. (*With her arms round* PAUL.)

PAUL (*shakes her off violently, in a savage paroxysm of anxiety, so that she nearly falls, shouting at her*). But you don't, you don't! That sort of talk means nothing! Nothing!

(*His violence is startling.* RACHEL *backs in fear, staring at him. His face is so ravaged and haunted that, for the first time, she does begin to wonder.*)

(*Quietly.*) You see . . .? You don't know what I am . . .

(*He turns away in despair and sits* R. *side of upstage crate.*)

Neither of us knows . . .

CURTAIN

ACT TWO

Scene I

A sunny morning two months later.
The room has been transformed by RACHEL'S *efforts—the books are all in place, there are new curtains, chair covers, lampshades, etc., flowers everywhere. It is now a gay, lovely room.*

      RACHEL, *kneeling* R., *is trying a costume she is making on* NANNIE, D.C., *who looks grotesque as Cassandra.*

RACHEL (*standing back and looking at her*). The trouble with you is you're quite a different shape from the captain of the second eleven.

NANNIE. He'll be missing his catches in this get-up.

RACHEL (*laughing*). He's playing Cassandra, not cricket.
      (RACHEL *crosses to* R. *of* NANNIE, *turns her round to face* L.
      There is a great clomping of boys' feet on the stairs and in the hall. We hear boys' voices and the slam of the front door.)

NANNIE. Oh, what a din! They ought to stay in their classrooms, if you ask me. Not come bothering in people's private houses.

RACHEL. It's only on Saturdays.

NANNIE. Saturday! I was nearly forgetting. (RACHEL *turns* NANNIE *back to face* L.—*pinning shoulder of tunic.*) Mr. Gardiner'll be wanting his lunch early. Catching the twelve-fifty as usual, is he?

RACHEL (*sighing*). I suppose so.

NANNIE (*glances at her*). He ought to take you with him sometimes. Make a nice change for you. Take you to a matinée or something.

RACHEL. He works all the time—in libraries—doing research for his book. He doesn't go up for pleasure.

NANNIE (*looking at her*). A little pleasure wouldn't do you any harm. You want to keep up your strength. It's time you started thinking about a family.

RACHEL (*faintly troubled*). Oh, I don't know about that. I'm not so mad about babies. (*Kneels* R. *of* NANNIE *pinning hem.*)

NANNIE (*horrified*). You? Don't talk rubbish.

RACHEL. Do you mind lifting your arms up? No, right up. Above your head.

(NANNIE *does so.*)
Well, it's not so simple you know, these days. It's not much of a world to bring children into.
NANNIE (*arms down*). It's the only one we've got, dear. You can't bring them into any other.
RACHEL. All the same, I expect there is something in what Paul says . . . The world's getting over-populated—dangerously so. It's no longer easy to know what to do about having children. Anyway, it's a pretty bleak prospect for them.
NANNIE (*turns to* RACHEL). Bleak prospect—I like that! What sort of a prospect was there for me, when I was born? Youngest of five, all girls, and father out of work all the time with his trouble. Nice thing if my parents had said to me "Emmeline, there's only a bleak prospect in front of you, so you're not going to be born at all". I'd have said "thank you" for that, wouldn't I? Thank you for nothing. I've enjoyed my life.
(RACHEL *rises to* R. *of* NANNIE—*pinning shoulder.*)
RACHEL. Dear Nannie, have you? I'm glad.
NANNIE. I don't say it's all been sunshine and roses. I've had me ups and downs, same as anyone. But I'm glad I was born, all right. And so's most people, if they're honest. Don't you go letting Mr. Paul skedaddle you into them ideas.
(CHARLES' *voice in the hall.*)
CHARLES (*off*). Anyone at home?
RACHEL (*pleased*). Daddy! (RACHEL *crosses up to* L. *below door.* NANNIE *follows to* D.L. *of her*, L.C.) Here we are. In the sitting-room.
(CHARLES *shuts door and comes in to* R. *of* RACHEL.)
CHARLES. Good morning, my dear. How are you? (*He kisses her.*) Good Lord, Nannie, what's happened to you?
NANNIE (*embarrassed*). It's for the boys' dressing-up, sir.
RACHEL. All right, Nannie, let's take it off. (*Takes tunic off.*) I can't really tell on you.
CHARLES. What on earth is it?
RACHEL (*crossing* NANNIE *to* R. *of desk, below chair with tunic*). Cassandra's costume for the Greek play. Paul's producing. He had to take it on because of Mallory's death.
(*Clomping and boys' voices, off.*)
NANNIE. There they are again—I'm sick of it. (*Exit.*)
(RACHEL *sits at desk chair.*)

CHARLES (*crossing to* U.R. *of* RACHEL). Appalling thing about that fellow —Mallory. Quite young, wasn't he?

RACHEL. Fifty something, that's all. Where's Mummy?

CHARLES. Having coffee with two Conservative ladies. I decided I was a Liberal!

PAUL (*off*). I must have those Virgil essays next time.

BOY'S VOICE (*off*). Is that next week, sir, or on Friday?

PAUL (*off*). I'd better have them on Friday. Then we can discuss them.

CHARLES (*quickly*). Everything all right?

RACHEL. Yes, darling. Fine. Fine.

(*Sound of front door closing.* CHARLES *turns* U.C. PAUL, *wearing academic gown enters, shutting door, crosses above sofa to* R. *end of mantel, crossing above stool.*)

PAUL (*to* CHARLES). Oh hullo! (*Looks for cigarettes.*) We haven't seen you for ages. How are you? (*To* RACHEL.) Darling, aren't there any cigarettes?

RACHEL (*in mock anxiety*). Oh my love, no nicotine? What an emergency! Wait a moment! In my bag. (*She finds a packet, gives him one and lights it with mock haste.*) Here! Here you are. Quick! Quick! We can't have you having a nervous breakdown.

PAUL (*laughing, kissing her*). Isn't she good at it?

CHARLES. What? Being the little woman?

PAUL. Yes. Have you seen the costumes for the "Agamemnon"?

CHARLES (*drily*). Well, I've seen Cassandra's.

(PAUL *inhales his cigarette deeply and sighs with satisfaction.*)

PAUL. Ah, that's better! That's the snag about being a schoolmaster— the number of hours in the day when you can't smoke.

RACHEL (*crossing to desk*). It saves a hundred a year.

PAUL. They're just the hours when one *wants* to smoke. Let's give the whole thing up, darling, and go and run an hotel in the Bahamas. Shall we? Lie all day on the beach, smoking American, mentholised cigarettes . . .

(RACHEL *sits desk chair facing upstage, picks up tunic and sews braid.*)

RACHEL. You can't run an hotel by lying on the beach.

PAUL (*to below stool*). We'll own it, then. You're far too good to be a schoolmaster's wife. Don't you agree, sir? She deserves a glamorous international air-line sort of existence—with a good solid spiv of a husband who knows how to—what's it called?—operate the money market. (*To* R.C.) Let's pack up and have done with ushering, eh?

CHARLES (*crossing above* RACHEL *and below sofa to sit upstage corner*). I gather the boys have been a bit stupid this morning?

PAUL. Stupid? (*He turns away to* R. *below armchair, frowning; suddenly depressed and preoccupied.*) As a matter of fact, it's been . . . an exceptionally good morning. (*Then with reviving interest, in spite of his gloom.*) It's exciting, you know, when boys you've been teaching for months suddenly get a grip of the language. (*Turns to* CHARLES, *growing enthusiastic.*) When that happens, something else happens. Something quite big. An actual . . . flash of communication . . . across the centuries.

CHARLES. I don't remember that ever happening in my schooldays.

PAUL (*crosses and sits on stool, downstage side*). Well, it doesn't often. But this morning . . . We were reading Catullus—wonderful raffish romantic stuff . . . Usually they stumble through it, fumbling for the words—might be a government white paper for all the fun they get . . . But this morning one of them suddenly started translating with real irony and point . . .

CHARLES. Irony? You encourage a sophisticated approach to the romantic emotions?

PAUL. No, no, it wasn't a love poem. Just one of those sleezy social anecdotes. Catullus back in Rome from a provincial staff job, broke as usual, succeeds in impressing a girl he meets with the number of his servants—till she asks him to lend her some. Collapse of Catullus. They're not his, of course. They're borrowed.

(CHARLES *laughs.*)

PAUL. An actual moment of experience like that, in the past, suddenly come alive . . . re-created in their minds—oh, more than that even—spoken, made articulate. They become articulate themselves in English through learning Latin. I'm sure they get a better grasp of their own experience—because their imaginations are awake . . . What about a drink? (*Rises.*)

CHARLES (*fascinated by* PAUL'S *enthusiasm*). No thanks.

PAUL (*crosses by* R. *of and below sofa to* D.C.). What's so interesting is they each get there by different routes. One gets there because he's got a crossword puzzle mind. Finds the language easy. Reads Latin as you or I read "The Daily Express". Probably gets about as much benefit, too. (*Crosses* U.C.) Another gets there because he's a poet. When he's puzzled out the literal meaning he can—well, recreate it in English. (*Crosses above sofa to* R. *of* CHARLES.) Another gets there like an actor—instinctively. He doesn't know what the hell it all means—but give him a clue to Catullus' age, character, set up—the rest seems to follow by flashes of insight. Often wrong, of course, but sometimes magically right . . . Oh, if only it wasn't all so important to them!

CHARLES (*puzzled*). Important? How do you mean?

PAUL (*crosses below sofa to* D.C.). For jobs. Earning their living. If only their future didn't depend on getting scholarships . . . (*To* L. *of sofa table and speaking across it on back of sofa.*) This damned examination system favours the crossword puzzler. He's the best scholarship material. But in the long run probably, the least real creative use. (*Turns away* L.C. *to bookshelves, foot on library steps.*) He can do it all without anything *happening* to him.

CHARLES (*to* RACHEL). You've married an enthusiast, my dear.

PAUL (*turns to* CHARLES, *smiling*). You mean a bore, don't you? I'm sorry.

(MRS. TRAFFORD *puts her head in at the door.*)

MRS. TRAFFORD. Ready, Charles?

(RACHEL *rises, leaving tunic on desk, crosses to* L. *of* MRS. TRAFFORD *by* L. *of* PAUL.)

RACHEL. Hullo, Mummy. Come in.

CHARLES (*rises to above stool*). You've just missed a most persuasive dissertation on the teaching of Classics.

(MRS. TRAFFORD *and* RACHEL *kiss.*)

MRS. TRAFFORD (*friendly*). It's no use, Paul dear. You'll never convert me. (*To* RACHEL.) Darling, you've finished the new covers (MRS. TRAFFORD *crosses above sofa, by* L. *of stool to below armchair.* RACHEL *follows above stool to sit* R. *side of stool, crossing* CHARLES.)—they make all the difference . . . Don't you think she's done wonders, Paul?

PAUL (*startled out of some gloomy reverie and moving* D.L.C. *to above desk*). What? Yes. Yes, of course. She's worked much too hard.

(PAUL *turns away. Mention of* RACHEL'S *work seems to annoy or depress him. Pause. Everyone slightly embarrassed. There is a knock at the door.*)

(*Almost angrily.*) Come in!

(LAMB *enters and comes to above sofa with a bag of household shopping.*)

LAMB. Oh, I beg your pardon. Am I intruding?
RACHEL (*rises, crosses* CHARLES *to below chair* R. *of door*). No, come in. You know my mother and father, don't you?
LAMB (*bowing*). Indeed I do, yes. (MRS. TRAFFORD *says* "Good morning" *to* LAMB, *then sits on downstage arm of armchair* R. *To* PAUL.) There's a boy waiting for you out in the hall. Worsley, of Field House.
PAUL (*going to the door*). Oh blast! He's not meant to come now.
  (PAUL *goes out, crossing by* L. *of* LAMB *and shutting door*.)
LAMB (*rests shopping bag on upstage arm of sofa, to* RACHEL). Oh dear, my daily woman made me a shopping list and I left it behind. I found it quite impossible to reconstruct its probable contents, as I don't think her mind and mine work quite the same way. Let me see now, what was it I came for? Oh yes, of course, to congratulate you, my dear.
RACHEL. On what?
LAMB. The news about Paul.
RACHEL (*blankly*). News? What news?
LAMB. Well, perhaps I'm anticipating. Like the newspapers. About the Sixth.
RACHEL. The Sixth? You don't mean . . .
LAMB. He hasn't told you! Oh dear, now I suppose I shouldn't have mentioned it . . . Premature as usual . . . But surely he would have told you, if . . .? Oh dear, I hope it's true . . .
RACHEL (*laughing*). But what *is* it?
LAMB (*puts shopping bag in upstage corner of sofa*). Simply that the Headmaster has offered him the Classical Sixth next term.
RACHEL (*overjoyed*). Mallory's form . . .! Oh, how wonderful!
CHARLES. Splendid rumour, I must say.
RACHEL. Oh, I *do* hope it's true . . .
MRS. TRAFFORD (*sceptical*). He'd have told you, surely?
RACHEL (*checked, evasive*). Oh, I expect it's only just happened.
LAMB. Perhaps the rumour should be amended. The Headmaster *intends* to offer Gardiner the Classical Sixth.
MRS. TRAFFORD (*impressed*). I'd no idea he thought so highly of Paul.
  (PAUL *hurries in and goes straight to look for a book on the shelves*.)
PAUL. Sorry about this. I'd better have a look at this boy's work, now he's brought it. (*Still looking for the book*.)

RACHEL (*crosses to kneel* C. *on sofa, speaking over back*). Darling, you must just tell us—is it true—about you having Mallory's form?
  (*Pause.* PAUL *frozen, his hand up at the shelf, does not turn.*)
LAMB (*steps forward to* U.L. *of sofa*). I seem to have made a slight blunder, dear boy. I came to congratulate you on something that apparently hasn't happened. There's a rumour you've been offered the Classical Sixth.
PAUL (*trapped, still not turning*). Oh! Is there?
CHARLES. It's not true then?
PAUL (*coldly, turning to him*). Oh, yes. Yes, it is. Quite true.
RACHEL (*going to* R. *of* PAUL). Darling, how wonderful! I *am* glad.
CHARLES. Well, that's splendid news! (*Turning to* MRS. TRAFFORD.)
MRS. TRAFFORD. Congratulations, Paul, dear. I'm delighted.
PAUL (*moving away from* RACHEL). It was nice to be offered it, yes. (*Goes to a file on desk and looks through it for a paper.*)
MRS. TRAFFORD. You haven't turned it down?
PAUL (*turning to her*). Not yet, no. But I shall.
      (RACHEL *moves* L. *to bookshelves, below library steps. He smiles at her. Pause. Everyone is puzzled, uneasy.*)
LAMB. My dear boy, you can't! No one but you could follow Mallory. You're—you're—in the succession. It's—it's—almost a kind of—of . . .
PAUL (*wryly*). Inheritance? (*Shuts drawer.*)
LAMB. Exactly. I happen to know what you thought of Mallory. I should have supposed you'd feel . . .
PAUL (*sharply, frowning*). I'm quite aware of all that, Arthur.
LAMB. Besides, there's yourself to think of . . . a chance like this may not recur. Turn it down and you'll stagnate for twenty years in the Upper Fifth.
PAUL (*laughing*). Oh dear me, no. (*Moves towards door.*) I shan't be here. (*To* RACHEL.) Darling, I'm sorry. This has been rather sprung on me. I . . .
LAMB (*pointing at him accusingly*). You've been offered a job at another school!
PAUL. No. I've come to the conclusion I ought to give up schoolmastering. I'm not really suited to it.
LAMB (*annoyed*). You? Stuff and nonsense! I beg your pardon, dear boy, but really . . . it's intolerable . . .
CHARLES (*quietly*). What are you thinking of doing instead?

PAUL (*recovering now that it's over; quite gay*). I don't know. Business of some sort. Fur coats for Rachel. Something . . . impersonal. (*Then with a touch of bitterness.*) Something that doesn't depend all the time on one's personal influence—one's personal quality. (*To* RACHEL.) Sorry, darling. We'll talk about all this afterwards. Don't worry, will you?

(RACHEL *shakes her head, dazed.* PAUL *kisses her on the forehead. Then, as he goes, laughing.*)

Perhaps all I want is a job where I can smoke all the time. (*He goes out, leaving door open.*)

LAMB (*crosses up to door and shuts it: turns downstage*). Oh dear, I'm afraid that was my fault.

RACHEL (*turns and crosses to* LAMB). No, he's been feeling—oh, I don't know—unsettled lately. I expect this offer just—tipped the balance.

CHARLES. You'd think it would tip it the other way.

LAMB. Ours is an appalling profession, you know. The only people who *are* suited to it inevitably feel that they've not . . . (*To* RACHEL.) Do you mind if I go back through the garden?

RACHEL (*preoccupied*). Do.

LAMB (*turning, as he goes, with a chuckle*). Of course, the kind of man who felt he *was* cut out for schoolmastering wouldn't be fit for anything. Oh dear, oh dear . . . (*Then sadly.*) Now there'll be no one to do the library . . .

(*He goes out through the garden, forgetting his shopping bag.*)

(MRS. TRAFFORD *crosses up to below door, crossing* CHARLES *and above sofa.*)

MRS. TRAFFORD. You'd really no idea of all this?

RACHEL (*dazed*). No. None.

MRS. TRAFFORD. Oh Rachel . . . how awful . . .

RACHEL (*making an effort, smiling*). Why? (*Turns away, crosses down and opens downstage cupboard—kneels by it.*) What's awful about it? Have some sherry?

MRS. TRAFFORD. No, darling, we must get back. I do hope it's all right.

RACHEL. Of course it's all right, Mummy. (*Shuts cupboard door. Rises.*) I'd love some fur coats. What's all the fuss about?

MRS. TRAFFORD. Well, it's rather extraordinary. Don't you think so, Charles? I mean suppose you'd suddenly decided to throw up the Civil Service—soon after we were married—without telling me?

RACHEL (*up to* D.L. *of* MRS. TRAFFORD). I suppose we're different. Our generation, I mean. I should hate Paul to feel he can't move hand or foot without consulting me.

CHARLES (*above stool*). 'm. It's not that. It's the decision itself that strikes me as a little odd.

RACHEL. You don't live in it, darling—preps, early school, roll-calls, exam papers . . . Anyone might get fed up with it all.

CHARLES. Anyone but Paul. We happen to know that he's not.

RACHEL (*sharply*). What do you mean?

CHARLES. You heard him just now—about Catullus. That wasn't someone fed up with teaching. I should say there's something else at the back of it.

RACHEL (*her control snapping*). Oh, for heaven's sake, need we have a thing about it? (*Turns away to library steps.*) God knows, one sees why people won't live near their families. One can't make the slightest move without a great public debate.

MRS. TRAFFORD. Really, Rachel, I don't know what's come over you these days. You're so touchy about anything to do with Paul. One can't open one's mouth. Come on, Charles.

(*She goes out.* RACHEL *follows to see them off.* CHARLES *stops her.*)

CHARLES. Don't bother to come out. The car's there.

RACHEL. Sorry about that. (*Smiles at* CHARLES.)

CHARLES (*looking at her*). You would tell me, wouldn't you, if anything was wrong?

RACHEL (*kissing him affectionately*). Darling, don't fuss.

(CHARLES *goes.* RACHEL, *alone, stares after him for a moment. Then turns back and sits down to sew at a costume. Soon she lets the work fall on her lap and stares in front of her, in despair.*

LAMB *enters through french windows.*)

LAMB. I believe I left my shopping here.

RACHEL (*preoccupied*). Did you?

LAMB (*seeing it*). Ah, yes. There it is! (*Crosses above desk to above sofa, picks up bag.*) That's why I had to give up wearing hats, you know. Always leaving them behind. I had to go back to all the places I'd been in during the day, looking for my hat. I had to live a great part of my life over again, so to speak, simply for the sake of my hat. One year, I remember, I lost fourteen. (*Moves by* L. *of sofa and sofa table to sit downstage arm of sofa, holding bag.*) Eventually my wife persuaded me to give them up. Taking into account the waste of time—which might otherwise have been spent in some remunerative labour—the convention of covering the head was costing me seventy-three pounds a year. Even in those days. Now with the fall in the value of money, it'd be more like—let me see, three threes are nine, three sevens are twenty-one—two hundred and nineteen pounds. And with income tax at—well, more or less half, one would have to earn, well, practically four hundred pounds a year, simply to wear a hat . . . (RACHEL *sobs. He glances at her, rises, crosses* D.C., R. *of* RACHEL.) Why, my dear girl . . . That was a shock to you just now, wasn't it? I wish I'd never mentioned the wretched business. I can't understand it. What's the matter with him?

RACHEL. I don't know, I don't know . . . Oh, well, I suppose I do but . . . I thought it was all right now.
          (*Pause.*)
LAMB (*very tentative*). I don't want to seem to pry, my dear, but—is it perhaps some private trouble between you? If you think I could be of any help . . .
          (RACHEL *shakes her head, smiling.*)
No? Ah, well . . . (*Turns to go.*)
RACHEL. Arthur, I'm sorry, but . . . it's to do with something Paul doesn't want talked about.
LAMB. Then, of course, you mustn't. Forgive me, my dear. Affection, I'm afraid, makes busybodies of us all.
          (*At french window.*)
RACHEL (*rising*). No, Arthur, please! . . . Come back . . . (*Crosses below sofa and by* R. *of stool to fire.*) I've got to talk to somebody.
          (LAMB *turns back and looks at* RACHEL *in horror. She is clearly desperate and paces about the room as she speaks.*)
I can't sit and watch while he lets it ruin his whole life . . . Of course he ought not to leave here. We all know that . . .But how can you help, if you don't know? . . . (*Turns to* LAMB *above* R. *of stool.*) It can't do any harm, can it, Arthur? For me to talk to you? Can it? Can it?
LAMB (*to* U.L. *of desk*). No, my dear girl. You must do as you think best. I shouldn't like to influence you in any way.
RACHEL. I don't seem to have any judgment left. It's all so intangible. There's nothing wrong, really. It all goes on in his *mind* . . .
          (*Pause.*)

LAMB (*putting bag on upstage end of desk, crosses to* C. *by above desk*). There's one thing perhaps I should be justified in saying: I am a man and I don't regard anything human as not my business . . . (*Smiles at her. Pause.*)

RACHEL (*crosses by* R. *of stool to* R.C.—R. *of sofa, abruptly*). Did you know Paul was adopted?

LAMB. But of course, my dear. I think we knew that, didn't we, when he was a boy here? Surely *that's* not . . .

RACHEL. No, no, of course not, when that was all . . . But now . . . Something rather unpleasant has happened. It was just before we were married. (*Sits small armchair* D.R. *facing* L.) Paul found out that his father was hanged for murder.

LAMB. Oh, my dear . . . Oh, poor boy, yes . . . Yes, I do see . . . (*Then, eagerly.*) Dear me, though, how extremely interesting. (*Crosses below sofa to sit downstage corner facing* RACHEL.) Was it a—a well-known murder? Should I have read about it in the papers at the time?

RACHEL (*amused*). Do you always read the murders?

LAMB. Of course. Murder is, after all, one of the poles of human experience—not quite so interesting as suicide, perhaps, but still . . . Yes. It is, I suppose, the ultimate sin . . . I don't know why one should be ashamed of being interested in that—one ought to be, I think. What was the story?

RACHEL. We don't know. Paul's tried to find out but—it's not so easy. You have to apply to the courts. They won't grant permission to look at the records unless there's money involved. Anyway, not knowing has become a sort of obsession with him.

LAMB (*nodding*). I can see how it might.

RACHEL. You know he goes up to London every Saturday?

LAMB. Yes. His book sounds most interesting.

RACHEL. There's no book. He's searching through the files of newspapers . . . to find out about himself.

(*Pause.* PAUL, *who has shed his gown, comes in. He senses an atmosphere of constraint and looks from one to the other.* RACHEL *rises, crosses below sofa and* LAMB *to desk.*)

PAUL (*clipped, tense, deliberately light*). Ah! It was bound to happen sooner or later. (*Crosses up library steps to replace book.*)

RACHEL. What?

(LAMB *rises to* L. *of armchair* R.)

PAUL. No, no. Don't get up.
(RACHEL *moves between desk chair and desk and picks up costume.*)
RACHEL. Paul, I'm sorry, I . . .
PAUL. Don't worry, darling. It doesn't matter in the least. (RACHEL *sits in desk chair. To* LAMB.) Now you see why I'm leaving.
LAMB. No, I don't. Why on earth need it affect your position here?
PAUL (*laughs, takes pipe from pocket, comes down steps to* C.). They'd hardly be likely to employ me if they knew.
LAMB. Why should they know?
PAUL (*crosses above sofa and stool for pipe cleaner from jar* L. *end of mantel*). I'm afraid I shouldn't care to hang on to my job by concealing a serious disqualification.
LAMB (*crosses below* PAUL *and stool to* L. *end of stool, above it*). But it's not . . . Oh, I agree, some foolish people might think so . . .
PAUL (*sharply*). How can you be so sure they're foolish? Does heredity count for nothing?
LAMB. Well, no, I wouldn't say that, but . . . We don't know how these things work.
PAUL. If you'd spent the last two months as I have, sifting the filthy rinsings of the Assize Courts for traces of your father . . . And, my God, they are filthy, too—the rape in the cowshed, the child kicked to death behind the gas works, the old woman poisoned by her son for the lease of her house . . . And to be certain of nothing—but that one owes one's existence to a moment of desire in one of these brutes . . . these madmen . . .
LAMB. But, my dear boy, all life has evil roots. One is not an historian for nothing. The roses growing out of the dung . . . Dear me, that's an elementary reflection.
PAUL. Who was your father?
LAMB (*taken aback*). My father? Oh well, my father happened to be a country clergyman but . . .
PAUL (*laughing*). You see . . . ? (*Turns up to mantel, throws pipe-cleaner into fire.*) Oh, everything you've been saying is perfectly true, of course, but it's too general. It's the particular details that make the difference.
(NANNIE *comes into doorway* L. *of* LAMB.)
NANNIE. Your lunch is ready, sir. Better be quick, if you're going to catch the train.

PAUL. Oh, thank you, Nannie. I ought to have told you. I'm not going.
RACHEL (*rises to* L.C.—D.L. *of library steps, hopefully*). Not going?
NANNIE. There have I been running me legs off to get it ready! Oh well, never mind. It's all cold except the potato.
    (*She goes out, shutting door.* PAUL *fills pipe.*)
LAMB (*above sofa, turns to* PAUL). Very wise, dear boy. Leave it alone for a bit. It's a lovely day. Take Rachel on the river. I'm sure you'll both come to see the thing in proper perspective . . . You won't blame her for having told me, will you?
PAUL. I'm glad she did.
LAMB. I must say I shall regard you now with ever greater affection and—if I may say so—interest, than I have in the past. (*Crosses above sofa and below* RACHEL *to above desk: picks up bag.*) Dear me, yes. Certainly.
    (*He gathers up his bag of shopping and goes to the french window where he turns.*)
    A scandal in one's life, you know, can be a most—er—humanising influence. It can prevent a man becoming censorious . . . Not that you'd ever be that, I think? (*Cocks a quizzical eyebrow at* PAUL.) Would you? (*He goes out.*)
RACHEL (*crosses to* C.—L. *of sofa table*). You really don't mind?
PAUL (*above firestool, shrugs*). It makes no difference. We're leaving.
RACHEL. Do you pay *no* attention to what he said?
PAUL. He's a dear, kind old thing—that's about all it amounts to, I think.
RACHEL. But just now—when you decided not to go . . .
PAUL. I wasn't going anyway.
RACHEL. But what . . . (*Then slowly realising.*) Oh . . . you mean . . . you *know*?
PAUL. Yes.
RACHEL. But then . . . (*Crossing to* L. *of* PAUL *by above sofa.*) Oh, my darling, I *am* glad. Is it . . . very terrible?
PAUL. No, no, not at all really. Well, it's not . . . gruesome, if that's what you mean. It's odd, strange . . . (*Moves by* R. *of firestool to sit downstage side on it.*)
RACHEL. But tell me, first, how did you find out?
PAUL (*smiling, ironic*). Just stumbled on it in the course of my reading.
RACHEL. Last Saturday? (*Crosses by* L. *of stool to sit* C. *on sofa, facing upstage to* PAUL.)

PAUL. 'm. There was a child, ten months old, Paul Arthur: my names. And the date seemed to fit—nineteen-twenty. There was even a photograph of me—not recognisable, I may say—with my mother.
RACHEL. What was she like?
PAUL. Oh, all right. Except that the clothes of that period were so ghastly. They made every woman look like a murderess.
RACHEL. But . . . *she* wasn't, was she?
PAUL (*laughing*). No, no, one's enough in the family. He was one of those people who pose as having been squadron-leaders, wing-commanders or what have you. At least, they always seem to choose the Air Force nowadays. Then, it used to be the Army. Captain Ronald Smith, D.S.O., M.C. Ron to his friends. Good old Ron . . . Actually he'd never been nearer commissioned rank than batman to some M.O. at a base hospital. He spent most of the war emptying slops. A suitable occupation. In civil life he'd been in domestic service—with a pretty shady record. Excellent references no doubt, all bogus. The kind of undesirable manservant you don't want to get into your house. This'll please your mother, won't it?
RACHEL. Go on, darling.
PAUL. Well, after the war, in spite of his—er—decorations, he appears to have had some difficulty in getting jobs—or rather, in keeping them. One or two firms seem to have found out and sacked him: but didn't prosecute. Post-war sentiment about unemployed ex-servicemen. That gave him a bright idea—"a man of vision", as Arthur would say—he started an employment agency for ex-officers. United Kingdom Civil Appointments Bureau. I suppose he thought if he spent his time looking into other people's credentials, no one would think of looking into his. He seems to have been right. The agency did quite well. Nice fat booking fee and ten per cent of all the poor blokes' salaries for three years. Quite a racket. *And* all the kudos of doing something very like a charity. That's what he was at when he married my mother. She seems to have been a dupe, like the rest . . . Well, of course, it couldn't last. Eventually he bumped up against a woman who'd been a wardmaid at the army hospital where he'd been a medical orderly. She recognised him and threatened to expose him. He killed her . . .
(*Pause.*)
with an old service revolver that he'd bought second-hand and

carried about with him as a sort of stage property. Insignia of the officer class. It was probably the only shot he'd ever fired in his life.
(*Pause.*)
Through the back of the head. Late one night, up on the golf links. Presumably after an argument. That was the prosecution's suggestion. He'd been trying to get her to keep quiet and when he saw he'd failed . . . as she turned to walk away . . . he shot her.

(*He turns to find that* RACHEL *is crying. He goes to her and sits* U.S. *of her on sofa.*)
Darling, I'm sorry. I shouldn't have told you so abruptly.

RACHEL (*in tears*). It's not that . . . But you've known all this for a week. . . for a whole week . . . ever since last Saturday and I . . .

PAUL (*rises and crosses* D.R.). I had to settle this thing by myself. (*Crosses below sofa to* L. *of desk.*) I had to get clear in my own mind what we ought to do . . . before I involved you in it.

RACHEL. But why? None of this affects us, does it?

PAUL. I'm afraid it does, yes. At the trial there was a defence of insanity.

RACHEL. But, darling, surely, if he'd been—

PAUL (*moves to* U.L. *of desk*). Oh, yes, yes, it failed, of course. Legally he was sane enough. But medically . . . With such a history there's not much doubt about it, he was a psychopath.

RACHEL (*calmly*). Well?

PAUL. Well, for a start, we ought to think twice about having children.

RACHEL (*after a pause, coldly*). So that was it. I think you might have told me. Why did you have to pretend it was because of the state of the world, the likelihood of wars and so on.

PAUL (*turns to* RACHEL, *moves* D.C., *taking out matches*). All those things are true.

RACHEL. But they weren't your real reason . . . Oh, it makes such nonsense of all our talk. I tried so hard to see your point of view and . . . it . . . it wasn't your point of view at all . . . You were just—acting. All this week you've been acting.

PAUL (*defensive, ironic*). An inherited talent, no doubt. (*Lights pipe.*)

RACHEL (*kneeling on sofa and leaning over downstage arm*). Darling, this mustn't come between us. It never has.

PAUL. Nonsense. It always has.

RACHEL (*angry*). Then it's your fault, not mine. I've never let it make any difference. But you—you can't ever leave it alone—you let your imagination play over it all the time—till it becomes a morbid obsession. Oh, if you could only forget it!

PAUL (*drily*). I suppose you'd like me to forget my mother, too.

RACHEL. Your mother?

PAUL. My imagination plays, as you call it, over her. She may still be alive. No reason to think she isn't. (*Crosses up to sofa table, puts spent match in ashtray.*) She seems to have been quite fond of him, but she doesn't seem to have realised fully what he was till after the baby was born, when she found herself up to the neck in a murder trial. She gave evidence for the defence. It didn't amount to much. Ron always liked tea in the evenings. No, he was hardly ever out late. Oh yes, I should have noticed mud. Ron was always so particular about his shoes. A few weeks later, I suppose, he was hanged, and she was left—holding the baby. My imagination plays over that. Not unnaturally, I should have thought . . . She must be sixty now. Growing a little tired of earning her own living. Feeling a little lonely, I dare say, as old age draws on. Wondering sometimes —don't you think?—what has become of her son? Or are these the sort of speculations you consider morbid? (*Turns away* L.)

RACHEL (*distressed by his ironic, withdrawn tone*). Oh, darling, no! I didn't mean that . . . Oh, perhaps it is my fault that you feel I'm not with you over this. But I am. I do understand. And I want to help. (*Rises and crosses below sofa to* R. *of* PAUL, D.L.C.) Listen. I've had an idea . . .

PAUL. 'm? What?

RACHEL. Well, of course, you may not want to go so far as that—but couldn't we—oh, I suppose it wouldn't be very easy—couldn't we— find her?

PAUL. Oh yes, of course; I've put that in hand already. I've got an inquiry agent on to it. I'm expecting a report any day now.

(*Pause.*)

RACHEL (*turns away*, R., *disappointed*). I see.

PAUL (*glancing at her*). What's the matter?

RACHEL (*forcing herself to be cheerful*). Nothing, darling, (*Turns to* PAUL, *sits downstage arm of sofa.*) that's fine—fine. (*Smiles at him.*)

CURTAIN

Scene II

Late afternoon. Four weeks later, near the end of term.

PAUL *is alone,* R.C., *restless, waiting.* RACHEL *comes through from the garden with some flowers.*

RACHEL (*crossing above desk to door, puts garden scissors on table* R. *of door*). I thought I'd just put these in her room.

PAUL (*frowning, distressed*). Darling, I'm so sorry about this. It's infuriating.

RACHEL. It can't be helped.

PAUL. If she doesn't turn up soon, I shall have to go.

RACHEL. Could you drop these last two costumes on your way?

PAUL. Yes, of course. (*Impatient again.*) I never thought of her descending on us, out of the blue, like this.

RACHEL. You don't think there's—anything behind it, do you?

PAUL (*glancing at her*). What sort of thing?

RACHEL. It almost looks to me as if she didn't want us to go there and see her.

PAUL. I suppose if she's poor, she may not want us to see how she lives.

(NANNIE *comes in to* L. *of* RACHEL, *very flustered.*)

NANNIE. I've had the windows open all the afternoon but there's still a smell of paint in there. (*Snatching the flowers from* RACHEL.) Oh, these'll help. I'll do 'em for you, dear. (*Turns to go.*)

RACHEL. I'm sorry about the rush, Nannie. The wire only came this morning.

NANNIE (*turns back*). Another one with no thought for others. Everything done for them. Well, she'll have to put up with it, that's all. I'll leave the rest till I unpack for her. (*Turns to go, into doorway.*)

RACHEL. Oh there's no need for that. She won't be used to it.

PAUL (*frowning, drily*). Much better not, I should think.

NANNIE (*with a glance at them, taking it in*). Oh. Well, at least she'll see that *you* live nicely.

(NANNIE *goes out, shutting door.* RACHEL *crosses above sofa and stool to mantel for cigarette.* PAUL *crosses below sofa, flicks ash off into ashtray downstage end of sofa table, crosses back below sofa.*)

PAUL. Look, I'm going to cut this meeting.

RACHEL (*crosses by* L. *of stool to* L. *of sofa*). Darling, you can't! The end-of-term staff meeting. It's unheard of!

PAUL. Yes, well, I know but—I hate leaving you to cope with her alone.
RACHEL (*sitting sofa—downstage end*). I think perhaps it's a *good* thing. After all, it's a bit of an awkward situation—for her, too. At least I can make her feel I'm not hostile. She'll probably expect me to be.
PAUL. And what if you *are?*
RACHEL (*gravely*). No. Whatever she's like one can hardly not be sorry for her. Oh, I don't know—there might be all sorts of things— I can just break the ice for her a bit before you come.
PAUL. Well, if that's what you really feel . . .
RACHEL. I do.
PAUL. All right, then. (*Looks at his watch.*) I'll just wait another five minutes.
 (*Pause.* PAUL *moves about restlessly, crossing below stool and above sofa to* U.L.)
RACHEL. How do you feel? Excited?
PAUL (*crosses to* U.C.—U.L. *of sofa, above* RACHEL). Guilty, for some reason. As if I were going to be court-martialled. A curious queasiness in the stomach. Fear, I suppose.
RACHEL. I think I'm a little frightened, too. It's absurd. Nothing to be afraid of, is there?
PAUL. The truth, perhaps? Responsibility? I don't know . . . I feel as if something that had threatened me for years, in dreams, were suddenly here, in the room, alive . . . But not visible yet . . . (*Sighs.*) Oh, it's all nonsense, of course. (*Moves away* L. *and back to* U.C.) I wish we had more money.
RACHEL. What use would money be?
PAUL. Well, for heaven's sake! We can't have her to live with us.
RACHEL. What!
PAUL (*moving up and down* L. *of sofa*). Well, it may be awkward. She must be about retiring age. I may have to support her. Even on my salary here, I can't afford two establishments, and when we've left here . . .
RACHEL (*turning away*). We really—are—leaving then?
PAUL. It's been settled for weeks.
RACHEL. But he gave you till the end of term to decide.
PAUL. No man with a bad psychopathic heredity ought to be a schoolmaster.

RACHEL (*laughing at him*). My sweetest love . . . there's not the smallest reason to suppose that you're in the least like him.

PAUL (*crosses to* D.L. *of sofa below sofa table*). You and I have got to take a chance on that. But the people who send their sons to school here —why should they? . . . (*Crosses to below sofa, sits downstage arm*—L. *of* RACHEL, *puts arm round her*.) I'm sorry. You've worked so hard at the house . . . all wasted.

RACHEL (*cheerfully*). Oh, I can do that anywhere . . . I don't think you need worry about your mum. She's probably saved a bit. Buyers in these big shops earn quite a lot.

PAUL. We don't know that she is a buyer. (*Rises and crosses below sofa to* D.R.—*turns back at* R. *of small chair*.) She may be an ordinary assistant. The elderly one, with bad feet, at the glove counter . . .

RACHEL (*laughing*). Darling, you've got such a taste for the macabre.

PAUL (*amused*). That's not macabre. It's sentimental. I wonder how much bond there is between parents and children—apart from habit. (*Amused*.) I doubt if there's any reason to suppose we shall like her at all.

RACHEL (*laughing*). Never mind, darling, we can cope.

PAUL (*turns to* RACHEL R. *of her*). You're being so good about all this. You do know I'm grateful?

RACHEL. You don't have to say things like that. I don't do things *for* you—out of kindness. This is our life and we . . . we lead it. That's all. (*Rises, crosses towards door by* R. *of sofa*.) I'll go and get those costumes.

PAUL (D.R. *looking across stage out of french window*). Oh, Lord, here's *your* mother!

RACHEL (*moves back to* U.R. *of sofa to look out of french window*). Oh! Well, don't go without those costumes. Cope with her, will you darling, just for a moment—shan't be a second. (*Exit.*)

MRS TRAFFORD (*off stage*). Rachel!

(MRS. TRAFFORD *enters from french windows*.)

PAUL. Ah, good afternoon. Rachel won't be long. I'm afraid I'm just going out.

MRS. TRAFFORD (*crossing to above sofa*). I only looked in for a moment. I met Nannie out shopping this morning. She said your mother was coming to stay. I wondered if you'd like to bring her over to lunch to-morrow.

PAUL (*astonished*). Well . . . (*To* D.R. *of stool*.) thank you very much

but . . . Do you really think it's a good plan? I've no idea what she's like.
MRS. TRAFFORD (*appalled*). Then it's true—it's not Mrs. Gardiner. (*Crosses to* D.L. *of stool.*) Nannie said so but I couldn't believe it.
PAUL. Oh, I see. (*Crosses below* MRS. TRAFFORD *and below sofa to* U.R. *of desk, picks up folder.*) I must say I couldn't believe the invitation.
MRS. TRAFFORD. Well! I think you might have consulted us before taking a step like this.
PAUL. The step, as you call it, was taken by my mother. I simply wrote suggesting we should look her up during the holidays. This morning we had a telegram. She's invited herself here for the night.
MRS. TRAFFORD (*sits on stool, downstage side*). I'd no idea you were in touch with her—or even knew who she was.
PAUL (*crossing to* C.—D.L. *of sofa table*). I shall never understand the etiquette of married life. Does one have to get the permission of one's in-laws to get in touch with one's own mother?
MRS. TRAFFORD (*rises*). Really, Paul, that's a most unnecessary attitude.
PAUL. I don't think we'd better start describing each other's attitudes.
MRS. TRAFFORD (*crosses to* D.R. *of sofa to face* PAUL *across it*). Have you no thought for Rachel at all?
PAUL (*angry*). That's a question I find it hard to answer politely.
MRS. TRAFFORD. I'm sorry, Paul, but . . . how can you want her mixed up in all this squalor?
PAUL (*stubs out cigarette in ashtray on downstage end of sofa table*). Next to Rachel, if I have any obligation, I imagine it might possibly be to my own mother? Judging by the accounts of the trial, she probably needs all the help she can get. . . . (*Crosses towards french window to* U.R. *of desk.*) from me or anybody else.
MRS. TRAFFORD. The trial? Then—you know the whole story now?
PAUL. We do.
MRS. TRAFFORD. How long have you known?
  (RACHEL *comes in with the costumes. She shuts door and crosses* D.C. *to* R. *of* PAUL, *who comes upstage to meet her.*)
RACHEL. Here they are, darling. Sorry I've been so long.
MRS. TRAFFORD. Rachel, I'm horrified at what Paul's just told me. Your father's outside in the car. I think he should be told at once.
PAUL. Look, I'm afraid I can't stop. I'm due at a staff meeting. But Rachel knows as much as I do. (*To* RACHEL.) Sorry, darling. It couldn't be helped.

(*As he goes out with costumes through french window,* MRS. TRAFFORD *calls after him.*)

MRS. TRAFFORD. Would you please ask Charles to come in here for a minute?

RACHEL. Oh, Mummy, no! There isn't time . . .

MRS. TRAFFORD. He must be told. You don't know what you may land yourself in.

RACHEL. But this isn't the moment—just when we're expecting her . . .

MRS. TRAFFORD (*turns away* R.). I think it's a dreadful mistake to bring this woman here.

RACHEL. We meant to go and see her.

MRS. TRAFFORD (*back to* R. *of sofa*). I know, I know. You don't want her here, where you live, where Paul works . . .

(CHARLES *looks in at french window, crosses to* U.L. *of desk.*)

CHARLES. You want me?

MRS. TRAFFORD. Charles, it's true. It *is* his real mother.

CHARLES. Oh. (*He comes in, crosses above desk to* L. *of* RACHEL.) Hullo, Rachel, my dear. You look worried. Don't you want to meet your mamma-in-law?

RACHEL (*smiling*). I do, as a matter of fact, very much.

MRS. TRAFFORD (*impatient*). Oh, how can you? You know nothing about her.

RACHEL. We do know a certain amount.

CHARLES. What's her name?

RACHEL. Smith. Mrs. Smith.

CHARLES (*turns away to sit upstage* R. *corner of desk, laughing*). Oh, really . . .! If I were going to choose an alias, I should . . .

RACHEL. No, no, it's genuine. Paul's father's name *was* Smith. (*To* MRS. TRAFFORD.) *You've* probably seen him.

MRS. TRAFFORD. *I* have?

RACHEL. Didn't you know some people called Forbes-Grenville?

MRS. TRAFFORD. Years ago, yes. Ian Forbes-Grenville was a great friend of Cousin May's. We used to dine there occasionally for dances. Why?

RACHEL. Paul's father was their footman.

MRS. TRAFFORD. Well, I can hardly be expected to remember a f— Rachel! Not that dreadful creature?

RACHEL (*to* D.L. *of sofa, amused*). I expect so.

MRS. TRAFFORD. There was a case about it. He swindled them.
RACHEL. That's it. (*Sits* D.L. *corner of back of sofa.*)
MRS. TRAFFORD (*gives a little shudder*). Ugh, how revolting! Yes, yes, I do remember hearing all about it. He'd been a page at some London hotel and old Sir Robert took a fancy to him and imported him into the house.

(CHARLES *laughs.*)

Charles, it's not amusing. (*Sits downstage corner of sofa.*) He was an out and out criminal. It was ages before they heard the last of him—long after they'd sacked him, I mean. You see, he'd found out so much about them while he was in the house.

CHARLES. Oh—blackmail?

MRS. TRAFFORD. No—but he'd found out so much about them that he was able to go all over the place, posing as a member of the family—running up bills and that sort of thing. You remember old Lady Grenville, Charles, the dotty one who lived at Brighton? Well, I believe he got quite a lot of money out of her; passing himself off as an illegitimate grandson, I think! He even joined quite a good club. Oh, there was a whole lot more I can't remember, but Mamma always used to tell us about him to prove how dangerous it is to engage servants, without proper personal references . . . Charles, don't laugh. Oh, Rachel, my darling . . . You! Married to that creature's son . . .

(RACHEL *moves away* U.C. *impatiently.*)

CHARLES (*to* MRS. TRAFFORD). When was all this?
MRS. TRAFFORD. Soon after I came out. About nineteen eleven.
CHARLES (*to* RACHEL). And the . . . the other business?
RACHEL (D.C.). After the war. Nineteen twenty. He seems to have gone on living much the same sort of life. He set up in business, posing as an ex-officer. Someone threatened to expose him and he shot her.
CHARLES. A woman?
RACHEL. Yes. Her body was found in a pond—near a golf course in Surrey.

(*Pause.* CHARLES *sighs.*)

MRS. TRAFFORD (*with a shudder*). How loathsome . . . (*Rises to below sofa.*) Charles, you can't hear that and just stand there and do nothing.
CHARLES. It seems a little late to do anything.
MRS. TRAFFORD (*to* R. *of* RACHEL). Why did you ever let Paul get in touch with her? Couldn't you have prevented it?

RACHEL. It was my idea. I . . . wanted him to find her.

MRS. TRAFFORD. You *wanted* him to?

RACHEL. He was worried about her. It's only natural he should feel some responsibility.

MRS. TRAFFORD. There are ways of doing these things . . . He could have sent her money through . . . through solicitors or something, couldn't he, Charles? It's such a mistake to let her know where you are. Once you get mixed up with her, you'll probably never get rid of her. She'll be pestering you and sponging on you for the rest of her days.

RACHEL. He wasn't thinking only of money. (*Crosses* MRS. TRAFFORD *to* D.R.) There are other kinds of responsibility . . . To one's mother? Surely?

MRS. TRAFFORD. I'm realistic, that's all. I always knew a marriage of this sort would lead to trouble (RACHEL *turns away* D.R.) and it has. You can't pretend you and Paul are happy together.

CHARLES (*making a movement to restrain her*). Nina . . .

MRS. TRAFFORD. No, Charles, what's the use of pretending? Sometimes it's quite uncomfortable to be here; you're both so on edge. And it grows worse, not better.

RACHEL (*quietly*). That's another reason why I want her to come. I want to force this whole thing out into the open. (*Crossing up to fireplace by* R. *of stool.*) I can be realistic, too.

MRS. TRAFFORD. Oh, Rachel dear, (*Crosses below sofa to sit* C. *on it.*) I'm not heartless about this woman. No doubt her life has been very tragic but . . .

RACHEL (*to above stool, suddenly angry*). Then why do you keep calling her "this woman"? She's Paul's mother!

CHARLES (*crosses by* L. *of sofa and above it to* L. *of* RACHEL *to intervene*). Now please—please! Your mother's only thinking of you, my dear. After all, the . . . the . . . the world, the milieu, it all comes out of . . . blackmailing page-boys, dishonest servants . . .

MRS. TRAFFORD. She was probably some frightful, scheming lady's maid. They used to be fiendish, some of them.

(NANNIE *comes in, very flustered, disconcerted to find the* TRAFFORDS.)

NANNIE. The lady's here, Miss Rachel . . . (RACHEL *pushes* CHARLES *upstage, crosses him, to* R. *of* NANNIE.) I mean Mr. Paul's . . . you know, Mrs. Smith.

CHARLES (*crosses by* R. *of stool to* R. *of* MRS. TRAFFORD). Oh Lord, Nina, for heaven's sake, let's get away.
MRS. TRAFFORD (*rises, crossing by* R. *of stool to above it*). No, Charles, wait . . .
RACHEL (*turns to* MRS. TRAFFORD). No, please . . . do go. I'd much better see her alone. You'll only embarrass her. (*Turns back to* NANNIE. CHARLES *crosses to below armchair* R.) Where is she, Nannie?
NANNIE. Seein' about the car. She asked which was the best hotel. Well, I didn't know what to say . . . (*Peers out of door, then steps back to* L. *of it, holding it open*.) Oh well, here she is . . .

(MRS. SMITH *comes in. She is an extremely smart, middle-aged business woman, very self-possessed, obviously prosperous and successful. Her slightly common accent is camouflaged by real* savoir-faire *and humour*. NANNIE *goes out, closing door*.)

MRS. SMITH. I'm so sorry. I've just been settling where my secretary should go. We decided "The Blue Boar". Was that sensible?
RACHEL (*bewildered*). Yes . . . yes . . . it's about the best, I think. I . . .
MRS. SMITH (*moves in to* L. *of* RACHEL). You're Rachel, I suppose? How do you do? (*She takes her hand*.) I do think it's kind of you to have me like this, on the spur of the moment. It was a sudden idea. I was coming down to look at this business in Bristol and I thought, well, as I'm practically passing their door . . .
RACHEL (*trying to recover*). Wouldn't your secretary like . . . I mean, I daresay we could manage to put her up if . . .
MRS. SMITH. We don't want her here, do we? She'll be all right. She'll find herself a room somewhere. I have to bring her on these long journeys. It saves so much time. She takes dictation while I drive. (*Moves* D.L.C. *a step or two. She glances at* MR. *and* MRS. TRAFFORD *but still no introduction is forthcoming*.) My goodness, public schools are frightening. We've just seen the tortures of the damned. They ought to shut the window.
RACHEL (*still dazed*). What window?
MRS. SMITH. In that big red building at the bottom of the hill. It was belching great clouds of steam, and inside were hundreds of naked boys, yelling and screaming in agony. It was like a mediaeval picture of hell.
RACHEL. Oh, those are the showers . . . (*Pause*.) I'm afraid Paul's

out at the moment. He . . . (*Steps back, turns to* MRS. TRAFFORD.) This is my father and mother.

    (MRS. SMITH *crosses* RACHEL *to* D.L. *of stool, shakes hands.* RACHEL *crosses* D.C. *by* L. *of sofa.*)

MRS. SMITH. How do you do?

    (MRS. SMITH *crosses below stool to* L. *of* CHARLES, *below armchair* R., *shakes hands.*)

MRS. TRAFFORD (*freezing*). How do you do?

MRS. SMITH (*to* CHARLES). How do you do?

CHARLES. How do you do? . . . Well . . . this is quite an occasion, isn't it?

MRS. SMITH. You *know* who I am! That makes it all much cosier. (*Turns to* RACHEL, *crosses to* R. *of sofa, speaks across back.*) Well, my dear, I *am* glad to meet you. That's one hurdle over anyway.

MRS. TRAFFORD. Hurdle? (*Crosses by* R. *of stool to below armchair* R. *of* MRS. SMITH.)

MRS. SMITH (*turns to* MRS. TRAFFORD). I thought in the car, coming down, "Ten to one, the wife'll be the snag". (*Turns back to* RACHEL, *moves to* R. *of sofa.*) But you're not. I can see that.

RACHEL (*amused*). You've not had time to tell.

MRS. SMITH. Thirty years in the retail dress trade, dear. You get to know a good deal about women. It doesn't take me long to sum up a customer.

    (CHARLES *laughs.*)

(*Turns to* CHARLES, *stepping downstage.*) No, seriously. Take your wife, now. The moment she came into the shop, I'd know she'd want everything sent on approval.

CHARLES (*highly amused*). You're right! She always does!

MRS. TRAFFORD (*defensive*). Well, shops always *used* to send things on approval. Before the war, there was never any trouble. Now it's always personal shoppers only and all that nonsense. And when they do send, it's usually some hideous colour you didn't order.

MRS. SMITH (*moves up to* L. *of* MRS. TRAFFORD). *We'll* send you things on approval. We make a special point of it.

MRS. TRAFFORD (*confused*). Oh . . . well . . . that's very kind but . . . er . . . Of course, it rather depends what *sort* of clothes . . .

MRS. SMITH. I know exactly the sort you like . . . Country clothes from Knightsbridge . . . Your whole shopping history's written all over you. (*To* MRS. TRAFFORD.) Leave it to me. I know exactly what you want.

MRS. TRAFFORD (*melting slightly*). Oh . . . well . . . that's very kind . . . It makes a great difference to have someone who understands one's requirements . . . knows the sort of things one wants. Well, Rachel, we'll be off now.

RACHEL. No, Mummy, do stay.

MRS. TRAFFORD. But I thought . . .

RACHEL (*urgently*). No! It doesn't matter now. I'd rather you stayed.

(MRS. TRAFFORD *looks at* CHARLES, *then back at* RACHEL.)

MRS. TRAFFORD. Oh . . . very well. (*Pause.*)

RACHEL. Well—let's all sit down. (RACHEL *moves up* L. *of sofa—indicating sofa to* MRS. SMITH. MRS. SMITH *sits* C. *on sofa, handbag down.* MRS. TRAFFORD *sits armchair* R.C. CHARLES *stands* D.R. *of her.* RACHEL *sits* L. *arm of chair* R. *of door* U.C.)

MRS. TRAFFORD (*to* MRS. SMITH). Did you have a good trip down?

MRS. SMITH. Lovely.

CHARLES (*crosses* MRS. TRAFFORD *to sit* R. *of* MRS. SMITH—*on stool*). I must congratulate you, Mrs. Smith. How did you know my wife always wants things on approval? It must be second sight.

MRS. SMITH. It's the secret of all business, really. Retail business, anyway. Knowing what the other person thinks, feels, wants . . . It's the secret of living, you might say.

CHARLES. I gather you . . . you actually own this . . . er . . . this shop, do you?

MRS. SMITH. Five. I've got branches in Manchester, Liverpool, Leeds, Birmingham and Harrogate. If this Bristol deal goes through, it'll be six. Not bad in thirty years?

(PAUL *enters* D.L. *through french window and stands* L. *of desk.*) Starting from scratch. Behind the counter. I hadn't a penny, you know. And all done by . . . well, no, not kindness, I'm afraid . . . by noticing people. Knowing just that much more about people than they know about themselves.

CHARLES. Here's Paul.

MRS. SMITH. Oh—

(*She turns to* D.L. *smiling and sees* PAUL *in the french window. She rises and stands* R. *of sofa, facing* PAUL *across the room. She cannot control the slight movement which the shock of recognition causes her to make. They stare at each other. Pause.*)

RACHEL (*rises and moves to L. of sofa*). Darling, here she is . . . your . . . your mother.

PAUL (*clipped, tense, with a little laugh*). Huh, curious introduction. I feel rather (*Looking round at the others.*) confronted by parents. A schoolmaster's nightmare.

MRS. SMITH. Oh my goodness, what a relief! (*They all look blank. She has to explain.*) That was a joke, dear, wasn't it? Not a very good one but still . . . That was the one thing that worried me about your letter. It was charming . . . but . . . just a little . . . solemn? I was afraid you hadn't got a sense of humour.

PAUL (*steps in to above desk*). Do you know where the mark lists are?

RACHEL (*to* PAUL). They're upstairs. I'll get them (*Going to the door; to the others.*) Then we'll have a drink.

(MRS. TRAFFORD *rises, crosses below* CHARLES *and above sofa to R. of* RACHEL. CHARLES *rises, crosses to D.R. below armchair.*)

MRS. TRAFFORD (*following her*). Rachel! . . . If you'll excuse me I'll just give her a hand . . . Rachel!

RACHEL (*turns*). Yes, Mummy?

MRS. TRAFFORD (*pushing her out, in an embarrassed whisper*). No, no. Outside. Outside. (*They go, shutting the door.*)

PAUL (*crossing below sofa to D.L. of* MRS. SMITH). *I* can't stop. I'm in the middle of a staff meeting.

MRS. SMITH. You came back out of curiosity?

PAUL (*amused*). Partly, yes. (*Pause. Then moving to her.*) Well, I suppose we ought to . . . er . . .

(*He is just about to kiss her, but* MRS. SMITH *repels him with sudden nervous violence, distressed for some reason.*)

MRS. SMITH. No, no, please. (*Recovering quickly, with a smile.*) See if we like each other first.

CHARLES. I thought you could tell at a glance.

MRS. SMITH. Well, in this case, there are . . . factors that . . . upset my judgment.

(MRS. SMITH *crosses above sofa, picking up handbag from upstage corner, to L.C.*

PAUL *turns upstage after her.*)

CHARLES (*going to french window*). Look, Paul, I've got the car. I'll just run you up there.

PAUL (*following him*). Oh—thanks.

CHARLES. No, no, when you're ready . . .

(CHARLES *goes out.* PAUL *below sofa and* MRS. SMITH *below library steps, look at each other. Pause.*)

PAUL. Well . . . here we are . . .

(*Pause.* MRS. SMITH *stares at* PAUL, *speechless. Crossing to* R. *of* MRS. SMITH, *opening cigarette case.*) Cigarette?

MRS. SMITH. Thank you. (*She takes it.* PAUL *lights cigarette with lighter from his pocket. She cannot keep her eyes off his face. As he lights the cigarette for her, her hand is trembling.*)

PAUL. I'm sorry about this. I could have cut an ordinary staff meeting —but it happens to be the end of term . . . end of the school year in fact . . . The fate of all the young gentlemen has to be decided— removes, examination results, syllabus for the next term . . . I can't very well not be there . . .

(MRS. SMITH *has been looking at* PAUL *intently all this time.*)

MRS. SMITH. What? I'm afraid I . . . I haven't heard a word you've said.

PAUL. Oh, it was nothing. Only that . . . I'm sorry to have to rush off like this. It's no way to meet one's mother for the first time.

MRS. SMITH. Not the first time, dear. We have met before, you know.

PAUL (*with a laugh*). Yes, of course. How absurd. One forgets.

MRS. SMITH (*her eyes riveted to his face*). We knew each other quite well, once.

PAUL. I must have been quite a different person.

MRS. SMITH. You were. Quite a different person.

(RACHEL'S *voice is heard calling from the hall.*)

RACHEL (*off*). Here they are, darling. You ought to go.

PAUL (*moving to door*). I'll be back as soon as I can. Make yourself at home, won't you? Really at home . . . See you later.

(*He goes, and meets* RACHEL *in hall, takes mark lists, kisses her, and goes out through front door.* MRS. SMITH *stares after him, stunned and bemused by the memories the sight of* PAUL *has called up.*

RACHEL *hurries in* D.L. *to cupboard to get out the drinks.*)

RACHEL. Oh dear, we've left you all alone.

(MRS. SMITH *is lost in reverie.*)

MRS. SMITH (*preoccupied*). It's all right, dear. I've been quite happy. I've been talking to Ron.

RACHEL (*turning, sharply*). Ron?

CURTAIN

ACT THREE

After dinner, the same evening. The room is empty.

LAMB comes in at the french window, carrying a thick sheaf of foolscap examination papers. He goes to the door and opens it. He hears MRS. SMITH'S voice in the dining-room and laughter from PAUL and RACHEL. He hesitates, comes back into the room and sits down to write a note, putting down the exam papers somewhere. The dining-room door opens. More laughter can be heard and PAUL'S voice in the hall.

PAUL (*off*). There are cigarettes in the sitting-room. I'll get them.

(*He comes in quickly, still with traces of laughter and gaiety about him. He crosses above sofa to R. end of mantel, picks up cigarette box, then turns to go out.*

LAMB rises to above desk. PAUL crosses above sofa to C.)

Arthur! This *is* nice. The very man! Come in and have a glass of wine.

LAMB (*uneasy*). No, no, dear boy. Really. I won't disturb you. I rather gathered you had guests.

PAUL (*crossing down to R. of desk*). One guest, Arthur. Someone I'd like you to meet. Come on in.

LAMB. No—really—I'd rather not if you don't mind—

PAUL (*picking up note LAMB has been writing*). What's this?

LAMB. Well—the Headmaster asked me . . . He wants another talk with you . . . He's very disturbed about your resignation.

PAUL (*drops note-pad on desk, crosses to below sofa*). Oh, why must he keep on like this? He knows the reason now.

LAMB (*moving in to D.C.*). He knows?

PAUL (*crosses up to mantel by R. of stool, puts cigarette box down*). Oh, for Heaven's sake, Arthur—the thing's settled! I've given him my decision.

LAMB. You don't want to go—you *don't*—you want very much to stay . . . Is there nothing any of us can do that will influence your decision?

PAUL (*bitterly*). No one can tell me I'm not who I am—Paul Gardiner. Alias Smith. (*LAMB turns away towards desk. Then laughing at him affectionately.*) It's all right, Arthur. Don't look so dejected. Thank you for the message but . . . There's no point in another interview. I'll ring him later and tell him so.

LAMB (*crosses* C.—L. *of sofa, shocked*). No, no, you can't do that. You must go and see him.
PAUL. Why?
(RACHEL *comes in, leaving door open.*)
RACHEL (*gaily*). Oh, hullo, Arthur!—What's happening, darling? Can't you find the cigarettes?
LAMB. I'm sorry, Rachel. I'm just off. (*To* PAUL.) Not on the telephone, dear boy, really, it's so rude.
PAUL (*laughing*). Nonsense!
LAMB. Don't you agree, Rachel? The Headmaster wants one more talk with Paul. Well, he can't just ring him up and say there's no point in an interview, can he?
RACHEL (*uneasy, glancing nervously at* PAUL). Oh . . . well . . . I don't know . . . I think . . . I think Paul must do as he thinks best.
PAUL (*bitterly*). Oh! We all know what that means! Paul's so insufferably touchy about the whole thing that I'm terrified to interfere. That's what you mean, isn't it? Isn't it?
(*Pause.* RACHEL *stares at him, terrified.* LAMB *watches them, appalled.* PAUL, *ashamed of his outburst, turns away then crosses by* R. *of stool to* D.R. *below armchair.*) I'm sorry. I don't want to do anything crazy about this, of course. I only want . . . (*He turns back to look at them. Then, with sudden resolution, happy because he really wants to stay at school.*) All right, then. I won't telephone. I'll go and see him in the morning.
(RACHEL *gives a little gasp of delight, then has a moment of doubt, going to him.*)
RACHEL (*crosses above and by* R. *of sofa to* L. *of* PAUL). Darling, is it all right? Is it what you really want to do?
PAUL (*very sure*). Yes, my darling, it is.
(*He smiles at her.* LAMB *watches them.*)
LAMB (*crosses down to above desk*). Mind now, Rachel, I rely on you— no telephoning!
RACHEL (*happily, with her eyes still on* PAUL). I don't think you need worry about that, now.
(MRS. SMITH *comes in quickly, smothering her amusement and leaving door open.*)
MRS. SMITH. My dears, your old Nannie . . .! I've just had the strangest . . . (*Then, seeing* LAMB.) Oh, I beg your pardon.
RACHEL (*crosses up to* D.R. *of stool*). No, no, it's all right. Do come in.

RACHEL. This is our neighbour, Mr. Lamb . . . Mrs. . . . (*Then to* LAMB.) I expect Paul's told you who it is.

PAUL (*artificially detached*). No, no, I haven't. Go ahead, go ahead.

RACHEL. Well, it's . . . Paul's mother—Mrs. Smith.

(LAMB *crosses up to* L. *of* MRS. SMITH. MRS. SMITH *to* U.C. *to meet him.*)

LAMB. His . . .? You mean his . . . ? (*Then, enthralled.*) Oh, good gracious me, how interesting. Dear me, yes . . . Good Heavens! . . . (*Taking her hand: gazing at her.*) *How* do you do? How *extremely* interesting . . .

MRS. SMITH (*amused*). You've heard of me, then?

LAMB (*embarrassed*). Well, yes, I have . . . I have indeed . . . I mean . . . Well, yes.

RACHEL (*above stool*). We've told Arthur everything. He's our best friend here.

LAMB. Dear Rachel, am I? Am I really? How nice of you.

MRS. SMITH. You're a master at the school, too?

LAMB (*looking down at himself ruefully*). Oh dear, is it so obvious?

MRS. SMITH (*laughing*). Well, my goodness, it's nothing to be ashamed of, is it? Education's one of the most important things in the world. (*To* PAUL.) Half the trouble with Ron was no education.

(PAUL *turns away* U.R.)

LAMB (*to* MRS. SMITH). I do hope you don't mind my knowing.

MRS. SMITH. I'm glad you do. I was beginning to wonder if we'd ever be free to talk this evening. There's always been someone here. (*She chuckles and lowers her voice.*) I say, what *about* your Nannie? (*Shuts door, crosses back to above sofa.*) I've just had the strangest conversation with her. You know when she came in to clear the table? Well, no sooner had you gone, than she started telling me how broadminded she was. (*Crosses below* RACHEL *and stool and* PAUL *to* L. *of armchair* R.C.) Does she think Paul's illegitimate?

PAUL. Oh, really!

RACHEL (*anxiously apologetic*). I *am* sorry. We ought to have warned you.

MRS. SMITH. It doesn't matter to me, dear. If that's their story, I thought, I'm sticking to it. (*Turns downstage, sits armchair.*)

RACHEL (*by* L. *of stool to* R. *of sofa, still anxious*). I'm afraid she got that impression from something my mother once said. And we've . . we've let her go on thinking it.

MRS. SMITH (*looking from one to the other, realising that there's a good deal behind this*). I see . . . Oh, well, people always think that about adopted children anyway.

PAUL. Of course. I used to think it myself. (*Crosses by R. of stool to sit downstage side on it.*)

MRS. SMITH (*interested*). Did it . . . worry you much?

PAUL. Not particularly. I used to fancy myself a rather romantic figure—the love child.

    (RACHEL *crosses by* L. *of and above stool to* R. *end of mantel for cigarettes and matches—crosses down to above* MRS. SMITH—R. *of* PAUL.)

MRS. SMITH. I often used to wonder what sort of story they'd tell you.

PAUL. I was left to make up my own stories.

    (RACHEL *offers* MRS. SMITH *a cigarette.*)

MRS. SMITH. And what did you make up? (*To* LAMB.) I'm sorry. This is such a bore for you. I'm brimming over with questions I want to ask. I know what's wrong with me. Thirty years of frustrated maternal instinct. Women *are* terrible.

    (RACHEL *lights* MRS. SMITH'S *cigarette, then crosses to sit* L. *arm of armchair* R. *of door.*)

LAMB. Oh, well, I'm afraid I'm old-fashioned. I'm a feminist.

PAUL. Arthur used to chain himself to railings in his youth out of admiration for the female mind.

LAMB (*crosses above sofa to sit* C. *on it*). Soul, dear boy, soul. Not mind. Go on. Tell us what you made up.

PAUL. Oh, well . . . At first, they were more or less fairy-stories. The emperor and the milkmaid—that sort of thing. As I grew older, they became more squalid—more realistic.

MRS. SMITH (*laughing*). How rude! There was nothing squalid about your birth.

PAUL. Well, you know what I mean. There was a gradual descent in the social scale. The emperor gave way to a drunken undergraduate earl who'd slipped up with a tobacconist's daughter.

MRS. SMITH. My father was a Nonconformist minister.

PAUL (*interested*). Was he?

LAMB. That must be where Paul gets his conscience.

MRS. SMITH. Has he one?

LAMB. Oh, very severe.

    (*They all laugh.*)

PAUL. Later on, when I was at school here . . .
MRS. SMITH. Were you? I didn't know.
LAMB. He's an old pupil of mine.
PAUL. In those days, I introduced an artistic Bohemian note—the touring actor and the landlady's daughter. There was a long period when I felt sure I was the son of an actor.
MRS. SMITH (*amused*). You weren't far wrong.
PAUL (*frowning*). Yes, well, so it went on. The stories kept changing as my experience of the world changed. When I was old enough to go about London by myself at night, whenever I was accosted near Piccadilly by a large middle-aged lady in fox furs, I always felt convinced that *she* was probably my mother.
MRS. SMITH (*looking at him, shrewdly*). 'm . . . I think it upset you more than you knew.
LAMB. I find it all so interesting. The whole history of literature in miniature. Starting with stories of kings, semi-divine emperors—
    (NANNIE *opens door, crosses down to* L. *of sofa table.*)
right down to the nineteenth century realistic novel, with its special interest in prostitutes . . . (NANNIE, *obviously hearing the last word, puts coffee tray on sofa table—goes out, shutting door.*
    LAMB *looks at watch.* RACHEL *crosses above sofa to* L. *of coffee tray, pours coffee, putting cigarettes and matches on upstage end of sofa table.*)
Yes, well, dear me . . . (LAMB *clears his throat with embarrassment.*) I must be getting along.
MRS. SMITH. I was hoping you were going to tell us something about Paul as a schoolboy. What was he like to teach?
LAMB. Well, I'm afraid I was boasting a little . . . (*To* PAUL.) You didn't come to me for very much, did you? One or two periods a week—for history, was it? (*Turning to* MRS. SMITH, *but talking almost to himself.*) But he had the heart of the matter in him—then as now . . .
    (*Pause.* MRS. SMITH *looks a little blank. He explains.*)
. . . imagination.
MRS. SMITH (*laughs; then drily*). That doesn't surprise me.
    (PAUL *gives* MRS. SMITH *a quick glance.*)
RACHEL. Won't you stay and have some coffee, Arthur?
LAMB. No, my dear, not to-night. You must have a great deal to say to one another. Dear me, yes, a great deal . . .

(LAMB *finds himself staring, fascinated, at* MRS. SMITH. *Then snaps out of it.*)

(*To* L. *of* MRS. SMITH, *crossing* PAUL.) Besides, there's a concert I want to hear on the wireless—a Brahms concert. (*To* MRS. SMITH.) Brahms is always—how shall I put it?—unexpected . . . and yet— somehow—inevitable. Like life itself . . .

(LAMB *finds he is again staring at her. He has taken her hand.*)

Yes, indeed, like life itself . . . (PAUL *crosses above stool to* L. *of* LAMB.) Dear lady, we shall meet again, I hope . . . Paul, my dear boy, I'm so glad . . . (LAMB *turns, pats* PAUL'S *arm, crosses below sofa and above desk to go out through french window. He goes quickly to hide his emotion.*)

MRS. SMITH. What a charmer! What an absolute charmer! Oh, how happy I am!

(RACHEL *crosses above sofa to* L. *of* MRS. SMITH *with coffee cups and milk jug.*

PAUL *moves upstage to* U.L. *of stool.*)

RACHEL (*amused*). Because of Arthur Lamb?

MRS. SMITH. No, no, no. Because of Paul and you and—well yes, Mr. Lamb, too, I suppose.

RACHEL. Milk?

(RACHEL *crosses back to sofa table, hands* PAUL *coffee.*)

MRS. SMITH. No dear, black . . . the kind of world you all belong to.

PAUL. It's the ordinary world.

MRS. SMITH. Oh, no, it's not, dear. In the ordinary world nothing counts except money—and doing one better than your neighbour— a bigger television set, a newer car, mink instead of squirrel. None of you are like that.

RACHEL (*crosses below sofa and sits downstage corner with coffee, laughing*). Well, I should hope not . . .

MRS. SMITH. You might have been. How was I to know? I couldn't tell what Paul'd be like. He might have turned out—well, anything.

PAUL (*with an ironic laugh*). Yes, indeed . . .

MRS. SMITH. A prig—that's what I was afraid of. I hate prigs.

(RACHEL *and* PAUL *both laugh.*)

PAUL (*puts cup on stool, crosses above sofa to downstage cupboard below bookshelves* L., *kneeling to open door, gaily*). I think we ought to celebrate. What about a liqueur?

MRS. SMITH. I'd love one.

(PAUL *goes to the drinks cupboard.*)
I thought in the car coming down—suppose they turn out to be the sort of people who don't have drinks.

PAUL (*at cupboard*). Where's that stuff we brought back from Italy?

RACHEL. Finished, darling. I don't think there's anything in the house.

PAUL. Oh, Lord . . .

RACHEL (*smiling, to* MRS. SMITH). We didn't know it was going to be this sort of evening.

PAUL (*rises and crosses to above sofa*). We didn't. That's what I want to celebrate. Do you like brandy?

MRS. SMITH. Well, yes, but please don't bother . . .

PAUL. It's easy, I can get it at the pub. Won't take a minute.

(PAUL *goes out, shutting door.* MRS. SMITH *rises, crosses above sofa to bookshelves* L., *putting cup on sofa table.*)

MRS. SMITH. Oh, my goodness, this is all so exciting . . . To think that all these books are his (*Then, reading titles.*) "Five Centuries of Greek Religion" . . . "The Silver Age of Latin Poetry" . . . Somehow I never thought of all this . . . Ah, here's one of yours —"A Hundred and One Mediterranean Dishes" . . .

RACHEL (*laughing*). No, that's Paul's. He's mad about cookery books. The French ones are mostly mine.

MRS. SMITH (*looking at more books*). Did he go to a university?

RACHEL. Oxford, yes.

MRS. SMITH (*meditative*). She did pretty well by him, didn't she? He's had everything . . . (*Sits on library steps.*) What sort of woman was she?

(RACHEL *rises, collects* PAUL'S *cup from stool, crosses above sofa, puts two cups on tray, crosses above sofa to* R.C.)

RACHEL. How d'you describe a woman who seems conventional on the surface but obviously isn't . . . can't be? Look at what she's done, how she's dealt with Paul.

MRS. SMITH. Yes. I thought any woman who'd deliberately take that risk must have something in her . . . I wasn't allowed to meet her, you know. No direct contact. Full information, of course. But information doesn't tell you what a person *is,* does it? Would you say that . . . well, that, on the whole, he'd had a happy life?

RACHEL. With her, you mean? (*Sits on small armchair* D.R.) Oh yes, I think so.

MRS. SMITH. Such a lottery this adoption business . . . I've often

wondered whether I did right . . . And then to come here and find that it's all come off—better than I ever dared to hope.
RACHEL. I suppose it has, yes.
MRS. SMITH (*rises, crosses to stub out cigarette in ashtray on sofa table downstage end, then sits downstage arm of sofa*). Of course, dear. *I* couldn't have given him all these opportunities. Not as I was then. He's made such good use of them, too. Oh, I feel as if I'd won the Irish Sweep or something.

(*Pause.*)

RACHEL. Do you really feel so much for him after all these years?
MRS. SMITH. For him? I don't know . . . I suspect it's for myself really. Wait till you've got a child of your own, dear. You'll know what I mean.

(RACHEL *turns away*. MRS. SMITH *notices*.)

MRS. SMITH. How long have you been married?
RACHEL. Oh, no time at all really. Not quite four months.
MRS. SMITH. Four months! You're practically still on your honeymoon.
RACHEL. Does that surprise you?
MRS. SMITH (*pensively*). I think it does. Yes.
RACHEL. We had to fit the wedding in with the school holidays, if we wanted to go away anywhere. We were married just before Easter.
MRS. SMITH. Where did you go?
RACHEL. Italy.
MRS. SMITH. Italy . . . What part?
RACHEL. Oh, all over the place. Venice, Naples, Rome . . . It was lovely.
MRS. SMITH (*looking at her shrewdly*). You didn't enjoy it one bit, did you?
RACHEL (*taken aback*). What?
MRS. SMITH. Never mind, dear. Honeymoons are hell.
RACHEL. Are they?
MRS. SMITH. A doctor friend of mine in Manchester always has to console the newly married ones. Apparently there's more anxiety neurosis among honeymoon couples than in any other section of the community. In fact, she says a honeymoon practically *is* an anxiety state. Well, it's only natural. You're both anxious to be at your best and any little thing that goes wrong, you think "My God, this is for life . . .!" Of course, I was lucky. I had a wonderful honeymoon.

RACHEL. You . . .?

MRS. SMITH. Oh well, of course, we didn't go to Italy or anywhere like that. Couldn't afford it. Ron wasn't earning very much Brighton was all we could manage. But Brighton can be wonderful, you know, when you're happy!

(*She is carried away by her memories and doesn't notice* RACHEL'S *amazement.*)

I'll never forget walking back along the front, late at night, after we'd been to a theatre or something, nobody much about, the sound of the waves down below on the beach and the moonlight slanting across the sea as if we had the whole world to ourselves . . . (*Then, seeing the look on* RACHEL'S *face.*) I suppose you're one of the people who think Brighton's an awful place?

RACHEL. No, it's not that. Only . . . were you really happy with him?

MRS. SMITH. Why not?

RACHEL. Oh, I don't know, I . . . When one knows what happened afterwards.

MRS. SMITH. Very few people'd be happy if they could see the future . . . I dare say I've always loved Brighton just because I wasn't happy very long . . . Of course, it depends what you've been used to. I'd never been about much, never stayed in hotels or anything like that. It was all new to me, new and exciting—hotel life, having drinks in the bar, eating in restaurants with the band playing . . . (*She laughs at the memory.*) Ron always used to be so amusing about the other guests. We used to try and guess what they were, where they came from, what their relationship was—oh, he made up all sorts of stories . . .

RACHEL (*amused*). Paul does that, too.

MRS. SMITH (*frowning*). Oh, well, that's different. With Ron, of course, it was more or less . . . professional. I didn't know that, though. I thought it was just a game. Afterwards, he used to scrape acquaintance with them in the bar, check up how right he was . . . I believe he did a lot of business that way . . . Poor Ron . . . (PAUL *opens front door.*) He was always at his best in hotels. That's how he started life, you know. Page boy. Clarges Hotel, Dover Street. Didn't tell *me* that, though. He used to make out to me that he'd been to a school like this. I believed him at first . . .

(PAUL *comes in with the brandy. Shuts door.*)

PAUL. Here we are. Sorry I've been so long. (*He shows* MRS. SMITH *the bottle.*)
MRS. SMITH. Very nice, dear. I always have that in the flat.
PAUL (*looking at her*). You know, it's extraordinary . . . You're so different from what we expected.
MRS. SMITH. What did you expect?
   (*Pause.* PAUL *puts brandy on desk.*)
RACHEL. Paul said you'd be the elderly assistant with bad feet at the glove counter.
MRS. SMITH (*laughing*). Why on earth should there be anything wrong with my feet?
   (PAUL *crosses to cupboard, gets three glasses and puts them on desk: opens brandy bottle and pours one.*)
PAUL. For the pathos. You were definitely a pathetic character. You know the kind—there's always one in a big shop—older than the others, grey-haired, marooned among a lot of teen-agers. One feels she's probably worked there for years. Tired out and a bit touchy. Her heart's bad, or she has arthritis, or something. One imagines her living alone in lodgings, with nothing to look forward to but a lonely old age and . . .
MRS. SMITH (*amazed*). And *you* got in touch with me—so that you could *do* something about all that . . . I thought you were just curious.
PAUL (*crossing to* L. *of* MRS. SMITH *with brandy*). Oh, we were . . .
MRS. SMITH. Of course but . . . You thought of me as that and you planned to look after me?
PAUL. Well, we . . .
MRS. SMITH. Oh, I *do* think that was kind . . .
PAUL. We're quite glad there's no need.
   (PAUL *smiles and hands her a glass of brandy. Overcome by this sudden realisation of their charity, she doesn't notice the glass he is offering her. Then—*)
MRS. SMITH. Oh, sorry. Thank you (*Takes glass.*) I don't know . . . I can't get over it somehow . . . (*She looks from one to the other of them. Then gives a little laugh.*)
   (PAUL *crosses to desk, pours two brandies.*)
Funny . . . I never thought of you thinking of me as—anything but what I am . . . Why did I have to be so dilapidated?
PAUL. We'd nothing to go on but the newspaper reports of the trial.

It didn't take much imagination to realise that being married to . . . to him . . . must have, more or less, ruined your life.

MRS. SMITH (*amused to see herself through others' eyes*). How odd it seems . . . Yes . . . I suppose I might have been like that. Actually, of course, it made my life . . .

(*Pause.* PAUL *and* RACHEL *are both dumbfounded.*)

MRS. SMITH (*warming brandy in her hands*). I've often wondered what would have become of me if I hadn't married Ron. I'd have had no life at all really. Not what you'd call a life . . . Running up and down stairs with trays for thirty years.

PAUL (*puzzled*). Were you a waitress or something? (*Crosses to* L. *of* MRS. SMITH.)

MRS. SMITH (*laughing*). No, no, dear. Mother was an invalid.

(PAUL *crosses* MRS. SMITH *to* L. *of* RACHEL, *gives her a glass, then sits* L. *of her on floor facing* MRS. SMITH.)

(*Then grimly, remembering something distasteful.*) Ever since I left school, I'd had to be at home—looking after her, running the house for father. If it hadn't been for Ron, I suppose I'd have gone on doing that till they died. I'd have been—let me see—fifty-four. I'd have had bad feet then all right.

PAUL. Well, but . . . you might have married someone else.

MRS. SMITH (*drily*). I never wanted to marry anyone else. (*Brief pause.*) Besides, you know, if anything had been different—even the worst thing of all—suppose Ron had just been killed in an accident . . . I'd have been back at that sink at home, sure as fate, for the rest of my days. *You* saved me from that.

PAUL. *I* did?

MRS. SMITH. They wanted me to go back, of course, but I didn't want you to be brought up in a place where . . . everyone would know. So I took you up north and got a job: two-pound-ten a week, selling hosiery.

PAUL. I must have been rather a nuisance.

MRS. SMITH (*laughing*). The trouble was to know what to do with you while I was at work. At first I used to leave you with the landlady. But when you were ill, I used to worry whether she'd look after you properly. So I stayed away from work. Well, they didn't like that, of course, and I couldn't afford to get the sack. It began to look as if there wasn't much future for us together. Then came the day when she found out who we were. The whole street knew within half an hour. That settled it. I saw what might happen wherever we went. And you'd soon have been old enough to understand . . . You see, I didn't mean you ever to know.

(*Pause.* PAUL *stares at* MRS. SMITH. RACHEL *tries to cover up.*)

RACHEL. You must have been awfully good at your job to do so well at it.

MRS. SMITH (*cheerful, matter-of-fact*). Concentration, dear, that's all. Of course, I was lucky. It was easy for me. After he'd gone (*With a nod towards* PAUL.) I'd nothing else to think of . . .

(*Pause.*)

And then I was lucky in other ways, too. Those years with Ron were such good training for business. I didn't know a thing about the world when I married. Not a thing. It was Ron taught me what people are like—how their minds and feelings work. And he knew a thing or two about people, I can tell you. Talk about salesmanship! Ron could sell you to yourself in half an hour! (*She chuckles reminiscently.*) And I was so shy. It was Ron taught me how to mix with people—manage them, persuade them, impress them. Right from those first days in Brighton . . . Oh, it was hell sometimes. He used to get so angry. "What do you want to be shy for?" he used to say. "Get people worrying what *you* think of *them*. That's the secret." It is, too. (*She chuckled again; then, sadly.*) Poor Ron . . . I didn't know, of course, why it was so important to him—me being able to impress people . . . But it's all been worth it, a hundred times over. I'd never have had the courage to set up on my own, if it hadn't been for him . . . Oh, it was an education simply to be with him!

RACHEL. How long were you married?

MRS. SMITH. Three years. Not long, was it? But long enough to go through the whole cycle—love, and birth and—death. There isn't much else, you know. There wasn't much—nothing, really—left out . . . Even happiness, I *was* happy . . . After years of dull routine, I'd been snatched into *life* . . . And ever since, I've had that reserve of experience to draw on.

PAUL. But the end—the end must have outweighed it all . . .?

MRS. SMITH (*suddenly grim*). No one can know. But when you've been down to the bottom, when you've moved about for months on the dark, filthy underside of the world where most people never go, when there's nothing worse left for you to learn or feel—well, you get a kind of strength from that, too.

PAUL. The strength of disillusion . . .?
MRS. SMITH (*matter-of-fact*). No. It's not that. It comes simply from knowing, absolutely for certain, what counts in life, what can survive—everything.
PAUL (*moved, looking at her intently*). I don't think you've the slightest idea how remarkable you are.
MRS. SMITH. Me? I'm very ordinary.
PAUL. No, no, you're not, you're not . . . (*Rises, crosses to* L. *of armchair* R. *To* RACHEL.) Come on, darling, let's drink to her! (*Turning to* MRS. SMITH, *enthusiastic.*) You're magnificent . . . Oh, it's all very well to talk about good coming out of evil: but it doesn't, you know. Not unless someone's got the power to transmute it . . . It's the only power in the world worth twopence . . . the only true magic . . . it's . . . it's human creativeness . . . (*He laughs.*) My God, it's extraordinary. I expected almost anything . . . But not to admire you. *Potnia meteer*—yes, there *is* something Greek about you. You've got all the clarity and reasonableness of Greece, the balance . . . *Potnia meteer*—yes . . .
MRS. SMITH (*rising, sits downstage corner of sofa, facing* PAUL *upstage*). That's Greek, is it? What's it mean?
PAUL. *Potnia?* No one quite knows. It's an ancient Greek word of respect, applied mostly to goddesses and queens. It's the stock adjective for mother in Homer—"revered", "august" . . . *Potnia meteer*—honoured mother! I salute you!

(*He lifts his glass.*)

MRS. SMITH. Oh, you're so like Ron . . .
  (PAUL *is held frozen, glass in hand.* RACHEL *gasps.*)
You *look* so like him, too. There! Now! Standing there with your glass. You might *be* him!
PAUL (*lowers glass, suddenly defensive, supercilious*). Really?
MRS. SMITH. Yes, yes. That, too! Everything you do and say . . . They say you talk, laugh, move . . . This afternoon when you came in . . . I . . . wasn't prepared for it somehow . .
       (*Pause.*)
PAUL (*cheerfully*). Well, we were just about to drink your health.
MRS. SMITH (*laughing*). Oh dear, and I interrupted. I *am* terrible.
PAUL. Come on, Rachel. What's wrong? Aren't you going to drink to your mother-in-law? (*Drinks.*)

RACHEL (*rises, crossing to* D.R. *of* PAUL, *dazed, pulling herself together*). Yes . . . yes, of course . . .
PAUL. H'm. Not bad, is it, this brandy? (RACHEL *turns away* R.) Not at all bad. I loathe austerity. (*He breathes in the fumes of the brandy.* RACHEL *sits armchair* R.) Oh, to be able to afford brandy every night!—the water of life . . . One quite sees why they thought it cured everything.
MRS. SMITH. Who did?
PAUL. Pretty well everyone—when brandy was first distilled.
MRS. SMITH. Oh, an advertising racket.
PAUL. No, no. Seriously. According to the best medical opinion. Half a minute. (*Crosses above sofa, mounts steps—putting glass on shelf: takes book from top shelf; turns downstage.*) I'll show you. Brandy was the great Tudor panacea. Much gayer than aspirin, don't you think? (*He comes back, finding his place.*) Wait. Yes. Here we are. (*He begins to read aloud, with relish and emphasis; picks up glass.*) "The Burning Water or Water of Life."
(RACHEL *and* MRS. SMITH *both laugh.*)
PAUL. "It helpeth *red* and duskish eyes. It is good for them that have the *falling sickness,* if they drink it. It cureth the *palsy,* if they be *annoynted* therewith. It sharpeneth the wit; it restoreth memori. It maketh men merry and preserveth youth. The smell thereof, burnt, killeth flies and *cold, creeping beasts.*"
(RACHEL *and* MRS. SMITH *laugh.*)
"It is marvellously profitable for *frantic* men and such as be melancholy."
(*More laughter from* RACHEL *and* MRS. SMITH.)
"It putteth away *fracins, ringworms* and all *spots on the face.*" (PAUL *shuts the book with a bang, and drains his glass.*) There! Now, if you'll excuse me, I must just go and ring up the headmaster.
RACHEL (*horrified*). Paul . . .
PAUL (*to* MRS. SMITH). Forgive me, I shan't be long.
RACHEL (*rises, crosses below stool to above sofa* R. *of* PAUL). Paul, please . . . please don't.
(PAUL *looks at* RACHEL *in silence and goes out, shutting the door.* RACHEL, *above sofa, rounds furiously on* MRS. SMITH.)
How could you? How could you?
MRS. SMITH (*bewildered*). Why? What have I done?
RACHEL. How could you say all that? About his being like his father?

(*Crosses her* R. *of sofa to* D.L. *of armchair.*) He's out there now—telephoning his resignation, throwing up his job here, his whole career, everything . . .

MRS. SMITH (*incredulous*). Because of what I said? But that's madness. Go and stop him.

RACHEL. No, no, it's no use.

MRS. SMITH (*rising*). Well, then, I will. (*Annoyed.*) It's idiotic . . .

RACHEL (*stopping her*). No, don't. Please. I dare say it would have happened anyway—to-morrow morning. But there was just a chance—and everything seemed to be going so well this evening. It's my fault—I ought to have warned you.

MRS. SMITH (*crosses above sofa, puts glass on sofa table, crosses to* L. *of* RACHEL, *firmly*). Now sit down, dear. You must tell me what this is all about.

RACHEL (*restless, not sitting*). I can't, I can't. Not now. He'll be back any minute.

MRS. SMITH (*impatiently*). Well, never mind. I can deal with him. Now, listen. You're exaggerating. Oh, he was surprised, of course, I could see that. But I don't think he minded. He was being quite gay just now about the brandy.

(RACHEL *crosses* MRS. SMITH *and below sofa to* D.C.—*turns back.*)

RACHEL. Oh, that's an act! That awful self-defence . . .

MRS. SMITH. Oh, it's all so familiar . . . (*Turns to* RACHEL. *Pause.*) He minds very much, then, about the past?

RACHEL. Desperately. He's never free of it for one moment. He pretends to be but he's not. It . . . it haunts him. (*Crosses to below sofa.*)

(*Long pause.*)

MRS. SMITH (*roughly*). Sit down. (RACHEL *sits downstage corner of sofa.*) Finish your brandy. (MRS. SMITH *crosses by* R. *of sofa for cigarette box and matches from upstage end of sofa table, crossing back to* R. *of* RACHEL.) Here, have a cigarette.

(RACHEL *submits.*)

My God, how angry this makes me!

RACHEL. Angry?

MRS. SMITH. Why do you think I ever let him go? Why do you think I kept away for thirty years? I meant this never to happen. What on earth possessed the woman? She must have been mad! (*Strikes match.*)

RACHEL. It was my family—when we were engaged. My mother.
MRS. SMITH (*wryly*). Oh, I see. The old appro. trouble. (*Lights RACHEL's cigarette. Pause.*) It's all quite recent, then?
RACHEL. Yes. If he hadn't met me, I don't suppose he'd ever have known . . . I just don't seem able to cope with it. The moment it's mentioned—"Quick, cover it up, let's be gay, let's be ironical, don't let's ever show what we feel". (*Glancing nervously at the door.*) We mustn't be found talking about him. He'll be so angry. Oh, you don't know . . .
MRS. SMITH (*looking at her shrewdly*). You're frightened of him. Aren't you? (*Pause.*) Yes. You are. I can see you are.
RACHEL. Oh, I don't want to be. But sometimes I can't help it . . . I can't get near him any more . . . I've managed to put up with it so far, because I thought it was all nonsense—his being like his father . . . But if it's true . . .
MRS. SMITH. Oh, it's so strange . . . it all happened so long ago . . . in the past . . . Even to me, who lived through it all, it's dead. But it's alive in this house . . . (*She sighs.*) You *have* made a mess of it.
RACHEL. I know. I know I have.
MRS. SMITH. Oh, not you particularly. Both of you together.

(PAUL *comes in with glass, very noticeably gay and exhilarated. He puts glass on sofa table, crosses to above desk, picks up brandy bottle, crosses to sofa table.*

MRS. SMITH *crosses to put cigarettes and matches on stool.*)

PAUL. There we are! That's done! More brandy, Mamma *mia*, more burning water. Away with fracins, away with melancholy! I'm quite sure you never have spots on the face . . . Where's your glass? Ah . . . (*He pours* MRS. SMITH *more brandy.*) Now listen. I'm full of plans. I want your advice. (*Crosses above sofa to* L. *of* MRS. SMITH, *hands her glass.*) You've put ideas into my head—filled me with commercial ambition! (*Crosses back to above sofa table, pours own brandy, leaves bottle on table.*) Why shouldn't *I* girdle the earth with chain stores? Eh? Why not? Possibly I've inherited some of your flair for business. One does—clearly—inherit things. Why not that? Do you think I'd be any good in the rag trade? Suppose I came to you for a job, would you take me on? (*Drinks.*)

(RACHEL *gets up and hurries to the door, crossing by* R. *of sofa. She goes quickly out, leaving door open. Pause.*)

PAUL (*puts glass on sofa table, crosses up to door, concerned*). I'm so sorry. I must just go and see that she's all right.

MRS. SMITH (*with a bitter laugh*). You're the last person.

PAUL (*turning sharply at the door*). What? (*Shuts door, coming back into the room, coldly.*) What do you mean?

MRS. SMITH. You can't do her any good because you're the trouble. Why is she upset now? Because I said you were like your father.

PAUL (*bitterly*). Is that surprising? It was hardly tactful of you. (*Turns away* L.C.)

MRS. SMITH. I should certainly never have said it if I'd known how true it was.

(*Pause.* PAUL *is taken aback.*)

PAUL (*turns back*). You can't have supposed it would be pleasant news for her.

MRS. SMITH. Or for you, I gather.

PAUL. I've always been prepared for something of this sort. But not Rachel. (*Crosses* D.L. *to above desk.*) She's never been quite realistic about it—always imagined one could ignore it. One can't, of course. The only thing to do is to face the facts and accept them.

MRS. SMITH. And you think you've done that?

PAUL. Certainly.

MRS. SMITH. Haven't you just turned in your job here?

PAUL. I had to do that.

MRS. SMITH. But why?

PAUL (*crossing to* D.L. *of sofa, he speaks across it*). Teaching's not like selling hats, you know. When you go to buy a hat, it doesn't matter a damn who sells it to you. But when you send your son to be educated—and by educated I don't mean just crammed with facts—I mean having his mind opened up, so that he can understand the facts, judge them, use them—having his whole character and personality deliberately subjected to influences—if education means that, then obviously it matters very much indeed who does the educating.

MRS. SMITH. Exactly. That's why you must do it—and people like you.

(PAUL *turns away impatiently to above desk*—R. *of it.*)

(*Crosses to* R. *of sofa.*) You'd be no good at business. You despise it. You're only playing with the idea of turning to business *because* you despise it, because you think it doesn't matter a damn. But education . . . One's only got to hear you talk, to know at once, it's your vocation—the only thing you care about, isn't it?

PAUL (*with a shrug*). Well, that can't be helped.
MRS. SMITH. Oh, yes, it can. I'm not going to let you do this.
PAUL (*turning on her, supercilious*). Well, really . . .! I'm afraid you must leave a professional decision of this sort to me.
MRS. SMITH (*angry*). Professional decision my foot! (*Kneels on sofa, puts glass on sofa table.*) It's an emotional decision. Throwing your career away because you've got in a panic.
PAUL (*impatiently*). Nonsense.
MRS. SMITH (*looking at him intently, musing*). Ron got in a panic, too—just like this—and fired a gun . . . But that's not really what frightens you, is it? Not just the fact of killing . . . It's the word—the idea—murder . . . (*Rises to* R. *of sofa.*) Oh, I know . . . It trails behind it all the other murders you've ever heard or read of. It settles in your brain and grows and grows.
PAUL. No, no! That's over. I *was* like that. Before I knew the facts. But since . . . I've tried to look at them objectively. (*With a laugh.*) Scientifically, even. Twentieth century man groping for his fate in Pelican handbooks . . . (*Crosses below sofa to sit on downstage armchair. He laughs ironically.*) What else can one do? They tell you a lot about red hair and blue eyes and colour-blind rats—and exactly how unlikely you are to have albino twins. But when it comes to character . . . all they can say is that there's a breed of Kentucky goats who inherit a tendency to fall over when frightened. . . . And even that they're not sure of.
MRS. SMITH (*to* R. *of* PAUL, *laughing, in spite of herself, yet uneasy at his irony*). What are you talking about?
PAUL (*suddenly dropping the irony*). I'm talking about having children. There *are* family histories of insanity.
MRS. SMITH (*incredulously*). You haven't been worrying about that! My goodness, Ron wasn't insane.
PAUL. Not in the legal sense, no. I realise that. But in *some* sense . . . surely? Those defence doctors were pretty convincing. What was it they called him? A psychopathic personality.
MRS. SMITH. That was his own idea . . . If that's what's worrying you, you can put it right out of your head. Ron was no more mad than you are.
(*Pause.*)
PAUL. No? Well, if he wasn't mad, he was bad.
MRS. SMITH. Luckily for us all, that's not hereditary. (*Turns away* U.R.)

PAUL. You haven't read my little books. Savageness seems to be inherited by rats. Anyway, rats produce rats.

MRS. SMITH (*upset by this continual flight to irony, crosses down to* R. *of* PAUL). You mustn't let this . . .

PAUL (*interrupting, very serious*). Listen. (*Rises to* L. *of her.*) What was he, this man I so closely resemble? You tell me he was sane. Very well. I accept that. But so much the worse. His character came out pretty clearly at the trial. He was a monster.

MRS. SMITH (*reminiscently*). No, no, he wasn't. He was charming.

PAUL (*contemptuous, bitter*). Charm, yes! (*Steps back, turns, crosses below sofa to* U.C.) Charm was his stock-in-trade. That's very clear. Right from the beginning, when he was scarcely more than a child, what was he? A cheap fraud. (*Moves down to* U.R. *of desk.*) He never had a single relationship that wasn't fraudulent. (*Turns to* MRS. SMITH.) You were simply another victim. Only it didn't happen to be your money he wanted.

(MRS. SMITH *doesn't answer. After a moment* PAUL *realises with concern that she is almost crying.*)

PAUL (*stepping forward*). I'm sorry, I . . .

MRS. SMITH. No, no, you couldn't realise, of course . . . You couldn't know . . . but I . . . I loved him.

(PAUL *stares at her.*)

PAUL. Even when you knew—what he was like?

MRS. SMITH. I always knew.

PAUL. I see.

MRS. SMITH. Oh, not what he'd done, of course. I didn't know that. But I knew *him*. He wasn't like what you've been saying at all. That's not a man, it's . . . it's a newspaper story. People aren't like that—not when you love them. And that's what they really are. . . . Not what they seem to policemen, judges, newspapermen . . . (*Pause.*) I see what's happened, of course. You and Rachel thought I was saying you were like some insane, inhuman monster. But you're not. Such a man never existed. You're like . . . Someone who was very like you.

(PAUL *looks at her, then turns away to above desk.*)

(*Sits downstage corner of sofa facing* PAUL.) Don't keep looking at him to see what *you're* like. Look at *yourself*, look into your own heart, to see what *he* was like.

(PAUL *still has his back to her.*)

PAUL (*turns and looks at her*). You loved him. But what he *was* doesn't depend on that. It's a question of *fact*. You don't suggest he wasn't guilty of murder?

MRS. SMITH (*wearily*). No, no. He was guilty.

PAUL. Well, then . . . there must have been something wrong.

MRS. SMITH (*angrily*). Of course there was something wrong. Exactly the same things that are wrong with you.

PAUL (*startled into superciliousness*). Well, really! (*Jumps off chair, turns* D.L.) I hardly think I . . .

MRS. SMITH. You can't run away from this. You've got to listen. You're afraid of something that doesn't exist, that never did exist. But there *is* something to be afraid of. Something that's in *you*. Oddly enough, it's the very thing that makes you a good schoolmaster . . .

(PAUL *laughs ironically*.)

What you have in common with Ron *is* something good—or it can be. It's all a question of how you use it. Ron became what he was because he was *more* talented than other boys of his kind, not less. He was gifted, like you are. But his gift destroyed him. All along the line, imagination was his downfall. Don't imaginative boys here, at this school, pose and pretend and put on acts? Of course they do. But it doesn't matter. They're safe here till it's all over. But where was he at fourteen? A page-boy in a West End hotel . . . Out in the world, you know, that sort of adolescent posing and pretending doesn't take long to become delinquency, false pretences—crime.

PAUL (*looks at her, then sits at desk chair, turned away*). Yes . . . Yes, I see that . . . Unfortunately it begs the question. There must have been some streak of brutality, ruthlessness in him . . .

MRS. SMITH. He wasn't brutal at all . . .

PAUL. But imagination doesn't make us murderers . . . There must have been something else . . .

MRS. SMITH (*sharply*). There was—and that's in you, too. (*Leans forward over arm of sofa towards* PAUL.) Insecurity. *Why* do you think he killed that girl?

PAUL (*surprised*). Because she threatened to expose him?

MRS. SMITH. Yes. But not to the police. He'd very little to fear from the police, you know. There *was* dishonesty, of course, but not easy to prove. They wouldn't have had a case against him.

PAUL. To his clients then?

MRS. SMITH. No, not to his clients. Nor to his friends at the golf club. To *me*. She threatened to tell me.

(*Pause.*)

You see—he never could really believe that he was loved

(*Pause.*)

He was afraid that, if I knew the truth, I'd . . . (*Turns away* R.) despise him.

PAUL (*with a contemptuous laugh, ironically*). I congratulate you. You've made quite a presentable story. (*Turns away to desk.*) But doesn't it occur to you that you may be sentimentalising him a little? (*Then without irony, turns back to her—upstage turn—arm on back of chair.*) Aren't you sentimentalising the whole situation?

MRS. SMITH (*turning to him downstage, slowly, very angry*). What did you say? . . . You wait till you've sat in court and listened to the death sentence on someone you love—and you know that it's just . . . Use your imagination on that! Think what those next weeks were like. I had to go and visit him, you know, while he was waiting. (*Turns away* R.) There were no real grounds for appeal, we both knew that. The date of his death was fixed. Eight o'clock in the morning—with a double brandy. I noticed it didn't mention that in your book. And he was young. Only about your age. Our whole lives were before us . . . (*Pause.*) I took you to see him once. He was fond of you. I don't suppose you ever thought of that. (*Looks over at* PAUL, *then turns back downstage. Pause.*) I used to come away from the prison and see the people in the streets—it was spring, the girls were just starting their summer frocks—and I used to think: you're nice, ordinary, kindly people and you all approve of what's going to happen. You'd be sorry for me, I suppose, but you wouldn't lift a finger to alter it . . . (*With a shrug.*) Why should they, after all? . . . Wait till you've been through that and see what happens. It knocks the sentimentality out of you, good and proper.

PAUL. I'm sorry. I shouldn't have said that.

MRS. SMITH. And the uselessness of it! He needn't have done it. Because I knew . . . Oh, not the details of course, but I knew the kind of front he was trying to keep up with me . . . But I didn't dare tell him. He thought my love for him depended on my not knowing, on my thinking he was—oh, it sounds so silly—a gentleman. It was my fault it happened; I was too anxious not to upset him. (*Turns to* PAUL, *leans over arm of sofa*.) But I'm not going to make the same mistake with you. You're afraid Rachel can't love you because of your—origins. But I'm going to make you face up to them, admit your likeness to Ron, so that you can avoid his mistakes.

PAUL (*ironical and supercilious again*). That shouldn't be so very difficult; he was a murderer.

MRS. SMITH. And what does that mean? That in a moment of panic he did one idiotic, destructive thing. He destroyed not only the life of that wretched girl but his own life and very nearly yours and mine—the lives of the only two people in the world he loved. (*Rises and crosses below sofa to* D.C.) Don't you recognise that? Don't you see that in yourself, too?

PAUL (*turns away to desk, head in hands, a great cry of repudiation*). No! I deny it! You're pressing this preposterous likeness too far. Out of all reason.

(*Pause*.)

MRS. SMITH (*crosses to* U.R. *of* PAUL, *quietly*). Do you know when you reminded me most vividly of Ron? This evening when you'd been to telephone, and you came back. You were very gay and excited, full of plans for the future; absurd, light-hearted plans. Well, that reminded me of one evening when Ron came back like that. He was gay and light-hearted, too, more than usual. He was full of plans for the future. He got out a lot of travel booklets from steamship companies—he always collected them, they fascinated him—Tasmania, Chile, Peru, South Africa . . . He made me choose where I'd like to live. "Lima", he kept saying, "let's go and live in Lima". He was laughing a lot and excited—so that I knew something was wrong. But I didn't know what—until some days later . . . That was the night of the murder. Only half an hour before, he'd been pushing that girl's body into the water. He was reckless and light-hearted, because he knew he'd thrown his life away. And so did you to-night. (*Then suddenly, realising*.) This resignation of yours is . . . your murder.

(*Long pause. They stare at each other*.)

Ah, you do see! (*To herself, slight turn away* C.) I only hope it's not too late.

PAUL (*shrugging*). Oh, it's not too late. They want me to stay here.

MRS. SMITH (*looks at* PAUL). I meant too late for you and Rachel.

PAUL (*sharply*). Rachel?
MRS. SMITH. Poor girl, she doesn't know how to cope. She's frightened of you.
PAUL. Rachel? Frightened of me? Nonsense.
MRS. SMITH (*dryly*). She told me so herself. To-night.
PAUL (*slowly, incredulous, angry*). She told you she was afraid of me?
MRS. SMITH. She's been afraid of you for a long time.
PAUL (*bewildered*). But it's preposterous . . . There's nothing in me to be frightened of . . .
MRS. SMITH (*ironically*). Imagination and fear, dear. The most destructive combination in the world, that's all!
    (RACHEL *enters to* L. *of sofa, leaving door ajar. She tries to make a plausible excuse for her long absence.*)
RACHEL. Sorry I've been so long. I've been helping Nannie. Having a visitor puts her in rather a flap. (MRS. SMITH *turns upstage to* L. *of* RACHEL. PAUL *rises, crosses to* L.C. *below bookshelves.*) Am I interrupting?
MRS. SMITH. A very good thing, dear. I expect I've said far too much. Now, if you don't mind, I think I'll go to bed. It's been a tiring day. (*Turning to* PAUL.) Good night, Paul.
PAUL. Good night.
    (MRS. SMITH *crosses up to door and opens it.*)
RACHEL (*following her to the door*). I'll just come and see that you've got everything you want.
MRS. SMITH. Ashtray . . . reading lamp . . . you haven't forgotten anything. Good night, dear.
    (MRS. SMITH *goes out.* RACHEL *is just about to follow.*)
PAUL (*at bookshelves, downstage end, with back to* RACHEL). Rachel! Wait a moment! Come here.
RACHEL (*turning at the door*). I must just go and see that she's all right.
PAUL (*formidable*). Come here!
    (*Frightened by his tone, she shuts door and comes slowly back towards him. He looks at her searchingly, penetratingly.*)
RACHEL (*frightened*). Paul, don't! Don't look at me like that.
PAUL. 'm. She was right. You *are* afraid of me.
RACHEL. Oh no, no, please. Let me explain.
PAUL. You can't explain away that look, my darling.
RACHEL. I can. I can explain.
    (PAUL *crosses* RACHEL *and below sofa to* D.R. *above small armchair.*)

PAUL (*moving away, aloof now*). There's no need. The thing's not difficult to understand.

RACHEL (*moves* D.C.). There! That's what's so frightening! You're a million miles away . . . I can't reach you. You've lived through all this by yourself . . . (*Turns away towards french windows—above desk.*) Oh, I'm not the right person! You need someone different altogether, with more experience. Like her.

PAUL. One needs, unfortunately, only the person one loves.

RACHEL (*crosses* C.). But if you love the wrong *sort* of person—who can't help? (*Crosses* U.C.) Oh, the future terrifies me! If we're to be like this, what's to become of us?

PAUL (*lightly, but with bitter irony*). Well, if character is destiny, I suppose the pattern of my father's life will somehow repeat itself in me.
(*His smile appals her.*)

RACHEL (*moving up and down* L.C., *desperate*). Oh, I'm the wrong person, the wrong person! You ought to have married someone else. Not me, not me . . . !

PAUL (*crosses* U.R. *to below stool, very quickly*). Ah! . . . I knew the time would come when you'd reproach me for it.

RACHEL (*to* L. *of sofa table*). I don't reproach you. I reproach myself.

PAUL. Your manners, my darling, are perfect. But it comes to the same thing . . . Well, thank God we've no children. I shan't have done you any irreparable harm, if we cut our losses and pack up. (*Turns upstage away from her.*)

RACHEL (*almost inaudible but an anguished cry*). Oh no . . .

PAUL (*amazed, longing to take advantage of this but therefore all the more aloof and cold*). I don't understand. (*Turns back to* RACHEL.) You're afraid of me. I've seen that. You're terrified of our future. You say I ought not to have married you . . . Very well. I offer you a chance to escape.

RACHEL. But . . . I don't want to escape . . . I love you.

PAUL. Even if I am—like my father?

RACHEL. You're not, you're not!

PAUL. She makes out a very good case for it. Suppose she's right? You don't pretend that would make no difference? (*Turns away, crosses* D.R. *with back to* RACHEL.)

RACHEL (*to* U.L. *of sofa, desperate and angry*). Oh! You don't seem to *begin* to understand. Yes, yes, of course it would make a difference.

PAUL. Ah!

RACHEL. Loving you would become misery, anxiety, terror . . . As it is becoming already. You don't think I'm happy, do you? I've never been happy for more than a day or two since we married. You've never given me a chance . . . Oh, yes it can make that sort of difference—the difference between happiness and misery—but it can't make the difference between loving you and not loving you. Nothing can do that . . . ever.

PAUL (*turns to* RACHEL). Nothing?

RACHEL. Oh, God! I can't stand this! (*Crosses above sofa to* U.L. *of* PAUL.) Love, I'm talking about, love, love, love! Not esteem, not respect, not something you can earn by good conduct or lose by bad behaviour. Love isn't rational. It's something that *happens* . . . I don't love you for your sake, out of kindness, but for my own . . . No, it's not even that. I love you whether I like it or not, however much harm it does me . . . Even when you're aloof, ironic, frightening even—yes, even then—don't you understand? My heart turns over with love for you because of the way you laugh, or move your hands . . . For better, for worse . . . that's not a vow, it's a description. (*Turns away from* PAUL.)

PAUL (*stunned*). I . . . can't . . . believe it.

RACHEL (*turns back to* PAUL, *despairing*). Paul!

PAUL (*moving quickly to* R. *of her*). It's all right, my darling, it's all right.
(*He takes her in his arms and covers her with kisses.*)

Rachel, my darling, my darling . . . Forgive me . . . I suppose . . . I never . . . really . . . could . . . believe . . . it was possible.
(*Pause.*)

RACHEL (*holding* PAUL'S *hands, steps back to* R. *of sofa, smiling through tears*). It's easy, you know, really. It could have been, all this time.
(PAUL *sits upstage end of sofa,* RACHEL *sits downstage of him, feet up on sofa, lying against him.*)

PAUL. That's what you've been afraid of, isn't it? You say I've been out of reach . . . only because I've been terrified of what this thing might do to us. Just as *he* was . . .

RACHEL (*puzzled*). Who? Do you mean . . . ?

PAUL. Yes. Ron. And yet—there was no need. She loves him still.

RACHEL. Yes . . . (*Then she smiles at him.*)

PAUL. And he must have realised that . . . when it was too late . . . !

RACHEL (*in horror at the realisation, a whisper*). Oh, darling . . . !
(PAUL *kisses her and holds her in his arms to comfort her. Pause.*)

It's strange . . . I can't think of her as your mother somehow . . . only as *his* wife.

(*Pause.* RACHEL *gets up, and crosses by* R. *of sofa to above it.*)

I'd better go and see if she's got all she wants.

(PAUL *catches her* R. *hand, she turns and comes back to above him, laughing.*)

It's all right, darling, I'll be back.

(RACHEL *goes out.* PAUL *sits lost in thought.* LAMB *comes through the french window, looks round and spots the forgotten examination papers.*)

LAMB. Ah, there they are! Good. (*He picks them up and makes a face at them.*) There was a time when I looked forward to correcting the boys' essays. I used to think one would see what had been going on inside their heads. One doesn't, of course.

(*All the same his attention has been caught by one of the essays. He stands reading it.*)

PAUL. What would you say, Arthur, if I told you I'm going to stay here?

LAMB (*to* L. *of sofa table*). Then you'll be able to do the library?

PAUL (*bursts out laughing*). Oh, Arthur! You love that library like a child!

LAMB. It must have a man of imagination . . .

PAUL. I'm through with imagination. In future the young gentlemen in my form shall keep their noses to the grindstone of fact.

LAMB (*glancing at him sharply, frowning*). You're joking, of course?

PAUL (*amused*). You look quite annoyed, Arthur.

LAMB (*with asperity*). Well, it's so foolish, dear boy. To me that sort of talk is blasphemy. Without imagination how can we apprehend the simplest fact? . . . For me, I suppose, any day now, time must have a stop. Three-quarters of a century of reading and thought . . . and what does it all amount to? One sentence from Keats' letters—the only fragment I have shored against my ruin—"I am certain of nothing—but the holiness of the heart's affection and the truth of imagination."

(*Pause.*)

PAUL (*deep in thought*). 'm. The holiness of the heart's affection . . . Yes. I believe in that.

(LAMB *glances at him curiously.*)

CURTAIN

FURNITURE AND PROPERTY PLOT

ACT ONE

TABLE

On it:
> Pair silver two-branch candelabra with candles, blue and white jar with daffodils, two books, ashtray (small glass) and matches (upstage end).

Under it:
> Piles of books.

Over it:
> Large gilt-framed mirror.

ARMCHAIR

On it:
> Yellow cushion.

STANDARD LAMP (practical)

SOFA

On it:
> Two blue cushions, MRS. TRAFFORD's bag with compact (in downstage corner of sofa).

TEA CHEST

FIREPLACE

Mantel:
> Two small marble busts, lustre jug (C.), glass bowl with red tulips (between jug and L. bust).

Hearth:
> Fender, fire-irons, wire fireguard on grate, two Japanese etchings leaning against wall R. of fireplace.

SOFA TABLE

On it:
> Four coloured framed bird pictures.

Under it:
> Piles of books.

BOOKCASE

Shelves:
> Piles of books.

TABLE

On it:
> Six framed miniatures (in two piles), ashtray and matches.

Under it:
> Two piles books ("Aeschylus" with Greek written out and translated set on top of downstage pile).

PROPERTY PLOT

BOOKSHELVES
   Piles of books, fifty-box cigarettes with ten cigarettes downstage end of bottom shelf.
CUPBOARDS
   Four sherry glasses (downstage), upper shelf of downstage cupboard, two hock glasses (upstage) upper shelf of downstage cupboard. sundry glasses for dressing.
PACKING CASE—lid closed
   On it:
      Chintz curtains with wire,
PACKING CASE—lid closed
   On it:
      MRS. TRAFFORD'S coat and scarf, two rolls carpet.
CRATE
   Three unopened bottles hock (not practical), one bottle sherry (D.L.) and one bottle hock (U.R.), unopened (practical), small box, wooden box with bottle straws.
FRENCH WINDOW
   Curtain pole with rings.
TABLE (in hall)
   Six unopened letters (L. end), silver bowl with anemones (C.), tray with two tumblers, cruet, water jug, bread in basket (R. end).
ELECTRIC FIRE
   Plugged into wallsocket D.R.
TWO BOOKS ON FLOOR R. OF BOOKSHELVES L.C.
OVERALL FITTED RED CARPET.
OFFSTAGE U.L. TO R.
   Trolley with two places laid with mats, napkins and rings, soup spoons, large and small knives, large forks, spoon and fork for serving (NANNIE).
   Tray with two bowls and saucers with soup (NANNIE).
   Tray with casserole with two croquettes, tomatoes and carrots, two large plates (NANNIE).
   Tray with two coffee cups and saucers and spoons, sugar, milk and coffee in pot (NANNIE).
   One coffee cup and saucer and spoon (NANNIE).
   Pipe (PAUL).
PERSONAL
   Pipe, tobacco in pouch and matches (CHARLES).
   Two cigarettes in case (PAUL)—one for MRS. TRAFFORD.
   Clean handkerchief (PAUL).
   Corkscrew (PAUL).
   Tobacco in pouch and matches (PAUL).
EFFECTS
   Car arriving and door slam (U.L.)

ACT TWO

SMALL ARMCHAIR
> *On it:*
>> Cushion.

TABLE
> *On it:*
>> Pair of candelabra as Act One. Silver bowl with red roses, ashtray and matches as Act One.

ARMCHAIR (from ACT ONE)
> *On it:*
>> Loose cover.

STANDARD LAMP

STOOL

MANTELPIECE
> *On it:*
>> Artificial birds in glass case (C.), pair Staffordshire china dogs (R. and L.), empty cigarette box, matches, ashtray (R.), china vase with pipe cleaners (R.), silver table lighter (L.).
>
> *Over it:*
>> Three painted china dishes, pair large china groups (R. and L.), pair small china figures (top R. and L.), four painted china plates (two each side).
>
> *Hearth:*
>> Fender, fire-irons and guard as Act One.

LARGE WING ARMCHAIR
> *On it:*
>> Cushion.

SQUARE TABLE WITH DRAWER (from L.C., ACT ONE)
> *On it:*
>> Lamp (not practical).

SOFA
> *On it:*
>> One cushion, RACHEL's bag with cigarettes in packet and matches (downstage corner).

SOFA TABLE
> *On it:*
>> Bowl with white roses (upstage), ashtray and matches (downstage).

LIBRARY STEPS

BOOKSHELVES
> *On them:*
>> Books arranged tidily including one on top shelf with "brandy" lines for PAUL.

CHAIR
> *On it:*
>> Greek tunic, hanging over back (NANNIE).

DESK
> *On it:*
>> Inkstand with pens, blotter, red folder, workbasket with pins, etc. (downstage), bowl with roses and carnations (upstage).

WINE COOLER with flowers.
OVERALL RED CARPET AND FOUR RUGS.
OFFSTAGE U.L. TO L.
> String bag with shopping (LAMB).

PERSONAL
> Pipe, tobacco and matches (PAUL).

EFFECTS
> Boys' voices and trampling feet.

SCENE 2

Strike:
> Costume and workbasket, RACHEL's bag from wing armchair, PAUL's pipe, wine cooler with flowers.

Set:
> Red folder on desk, exercise book in desk drawer (both from U.L. to R. standby table), cigarettes in box on mantel, stool back on marks, flowers on desk change to anemones, flowers on table D.R. change to yellow roses, flowers on sofa table change to pink roses.

OFFSTAGE U.L. TO R.
> Two Greek costumes (RACHEL), mark sheets (RACHEL).

OFFSTAGE D.L. (french window)
> Bunch of flowers and gardening scissors (RACHEL).

PERSONAL
> Cigarette—lighted (PAUL).
> Handbag and gloves (MRS. SMITH).
> Cigarettes in case and lighter (PAUL)

ACT THREE

SET AND FURNITURE AS ACT TWO
> *Set:*
>> Cigarette (MRS. SMITH), in box on mantel, book with "brandy" lines, on top shelf L.C. (PAUL), library steps facing down-stage water in ashtray on sofa table.

OFFSTAGE U.L. TO R.
> Tray with three coffee cups and saucers, coffee in pot, milk and sugar, three spoons (NANNIE).

OFFSTAGE U.L. TO L.
> Unopened bottle of brandy—practical (PAUL).

OFFSTAGE D.L. (french window)
> Bundle of examination papers (LAMB).

www.ingramcontent.com/pod-product-compliance
Ingram Content Group UK Ltd.
Pitfield, Milton Keynes, MK11 3LW, UK
UKHW021840210426
5322IPUK00022B/382